NATURAL-BORN ENTREPRENEURS

NATURAL-BORN ENTREPRENEURS

BREAKING INTO BUSINESS OWNERSHIP

LISA PIERCEY
MD, MBA

Entrepreneur | Books

Published by Entrepreneur® Books, Charleston, South Carolina.
An imprint of Advantage Media Group.

Printed in the United States of America.

10 9 8 7 6 5 4 3 2 1

ISBN: 979-8-89701-029-5 (Hardcover)
ISBN: 979-8-89701-030-1 (Paperback)
ISBN: 979-8-89701-031-8 (eBook)

Library of Congress Control Number: 2025913437

Cover and layout design by Matthew Morse.

06-27-2025 3:18

To all the natural-born entrepreneurs in my life:
Your hustle, authenticity, and grit have inspired me more than you know.

RN BOR

TURAL-

BORN

RAL-N

ACKNOWLEDGMENTS

This book is built on the enduring influence of so many incredible people who have shaped, guided, and inspired me throughout this journey.

First, to David and our children, Claire, Lauren, Ella, and Luke—thank you for your steadfast support throughout my demanding career with its multiple twists and turns. Your love and patience have been my anchor, and I hope you feel the same encouragement, autonomy, and grace that you've so generously given me.

To my parents and grandparents, who raised me with a Christ-centered faith, instilled in me a deep value for both family and hard work, and taught me that success is earned—not given. I owe most of who I am to your influence. I have been blessed by your (and my sister's) modeling of successful small business ownership and showing me the importance of investing in the community.

I am indebted to the mentors and advisors who helped me make the transition from the large corporate world to the joys of small business ownership, especially Jim Mathis, Mike Regnier, Alan Hymowitz, Brian Adams, Kolin Holladay, Don McLemore, Phil Wenk, the Ferguson family, and many others who have been generous with their guidance and wisdom. A special thanks to Misty for her loyal assistance in keeping me organized, and to Ryan, my long-time executive coach and friend, for always helping me keep my head straight.

To my partners and fellow board members, Lauren Fielder and Taylor Perry, thank you for sharing your mergers and acquisitions experience with me and allowing me to discover the pleasure of professional colleagues turning into friends. Taylor, I am particularly grateful for your invaluable help with content proofing and editing.

Thank you to the team at Advantage Media/Forbes Books—Adam Witty, Harper Tucker, Olivia Tanksley, Alison Kilian, Annie LaGreca, Katie Smith, and Elizabeth Brueggemann—for making the process smooth and fun.

And finally, to the sellers and employees of the companies I've worked with and the investors and lenders who believed in my vision, I am profoundly grateful for your trust and partnership.

This book is a reflection of the collective wisdom, opportunity, and empowerment I have received from so many remarkable people who smoothed my path for such a fulfilling career pivot. Thank you for walking this journey with me—I promise to pay it forward.

ABOUT THE AUTHOR

Lisa Piercey, MD, MBA, is a nationally recognized physician executive with extensive C-suite operational experience across the healthcare ecosystem. A serial healthcare investor, Dr. Piercey serves as a general partner in multiple funds and is the founder and managing partner of Tristela Capital Partners, a lower middle market independent sponsor firm.

Dr. Piercey has successfully acquired three privately held companies and oversees a portfolio of $20 million assets under management (AUM), serving in both governance and operational roles in the senior living, specialty pharmacy, and worksite wellness verticals. Certified by the Institute for Mergers, Acquisitions, and Alliances (IMAA) as an International Mergers & Acquisitions Expert, Dr. Piercey offers deep expertise in healthcare strategy and operations to private capital markets, with a strong emphasis on growth and scalability.

Prior to her focus on healthcare investing, Dr. Piercey served as Tennessee's Commissioner of Health on Governor Bill Lee's Cabinet, where she provided statewide leadership in health policy and regulation, large-scale operations, and crisis management during the COVID-19 pandemic, one of the most challenging periods in modern healthcare. Leading up to her public service, Dr. Piercey spent nearly two decades as a senior-level healthcare executive, providing clinical and administrative oversight in large medical group and health system operations, where she excelled at driving strategies for access to cost-efficient care, particularly in underserved and high-risk populations.

She holds a BS in Chemistry from Lipscomb University, an MD from East Tennessee State University, and an MBA from Bethel University. Dr. Piercey is board certified in both general pediatrics and child abuse pediatrics and continues to evaluate children who are suspected victims of child abuse and neglect. In her personal capacity, she provides executive committee leadership on the Board of Trustees for Lipscomb University, serves as a strategic advisor for both a Nashville-based healthcare venture capital firm and a private bank, and volunteers on the boards of several nonprofit organizations. Dr. Piercey and her husband, David, live in rural West Tennessee and have four young adult children.

CONTENTS

INTRODUCTION

A DIFFERENT KIND OF ENTREPRENEUR

***"To everything there is a season, and a time for every purpose under heaven."*[1]**

—Ecclesiastes 3:1 (New King James Version)

I get it—I have been there. I know that proud but oddly unfulfilling feeling of climbing the corporate ranks and feeling like you have yet to arrive, despite having impressive titles and a healthy salary. I understand how frustrating it is to feel constrained by bureaucracy and only be able to exact incremental, instead of monumental, change. I know how wearisome it gets to execute someone else's vision when your passion lies elsewhere. You start wondering, *Is this it—forever?*

That is the question I had to answer when I came to a crossroads in my career. The point of decision came after my term as Tennessee's Commissioner of Health—the state's top doctor—during one of the most challenging periods in modern healthcare, the COVID-19

1 Ecclesiastes 3:1 (New King James Version).

pandemic. As my term concluded, I had to choose which corporate ladder to climb again; I knew I wanted it to be the one with the most autonomy and alignment with my own vision and personal mission. Maybe it was the renewed sense of urgency and possibility that many of us felt after those tough times, but I knew I couldn't go back to the hamster wheel, which felt like an endless race going nowhere. I was ready for something with more purpose, momentum, and freedom.

As a physician turned hospital administrator, I naturally assumed that after my public service on Governor Bill Lee's Cabinet, I would return to hospital management. When the time came, I was fortunate to have numerous opportunities to reenter the private sector—some of them lucrative, high-profile roles that I once would have considered a dream. Yet, as I explored each option, I struggled to feel the expected excitement. The thought of stepping back into a large organization felt stifling. I realized that what I truly wanted was to carve my own path and embrace the entrepreneurial instincts that had always been in me.

Looking back on my career, I deeply value the roles I had the privilege to serve in. I learned invaluable lessons from many great bosses—and even a few challenging ones. I cherished the teams I led and the people who worked alongside me. But I also recognized a pattern: My success had always come from thinking differently, from thriving as a big fish in a small pond rather than striving to be first among equals. That realization pushed me toward a new chapter—one in which I could build something of my own.

I knew I had to own a business—not because I had all the answers, but because I wanted all the responsibility, as well as all the rewards, if I earned them. I considered launching a start-up, but with a professional lifestyle to support and four teenagers soon to enter college, I could not tolerate three to five years of scarcity while I got a new business off the ground. So, I decided to buy an existing business.

This way, I could (mostly) skip the hard part and take on an already profitable business that I could mold into my own.

I did not realize it at the time, but I was pursuing entrepreneurship through acquisition (ETA). It was a new concept to me—as it may be to you—but in fact, elite business schools around the world have been developing ETA programs for decades. But since I wasn't a twenty-something recent MBA grad, was there a place for me? As it turned out, yes.

As a mid-careerist, I found my path to ETA through a traditional search fund—one of the many ways of acquiring an existing business. There are multiple avenues to ETA, and all of those roads can lead entrepreneurial-minded, experienced professionals to the same destination of autonomy and financial security while enjoying the intellectual stimulation of a self-driven business adventure.

If you want to break free from the confines of the corporate world, ETA could be the right fit for you. This guide is intended to teach you how to acquire a small or medium-sized business and is written specifically for the non–business school graduate, although those with MBAs might benefit from this overview as well. Despite formal training in graduate school on finance, business operations, and mergers and acquisitions (M&A), most are still unprepared for sourcing, pursuing, and acquiring a small business. I have an MBA myself, and it was still a steep learning curve.

After being introduced to the concept of ETA by an investor friend, I launched an institutionally sponsored search fund and bought my first company. In two years, I acquired three health-related companies—in the areas of senior living, specialty pharmacy, and worksite wellness. Each one was acquired through a different investment model, giving me a wide range of experience in the many avenues to ETA, including a traditional search fund, a self-funded search, and as an independent sponsor. I raised nearly $20 million in financing for these deals, including investor equity, traditional and mezzanine debt, and seller financing, and encountered a wide variety of transaction challenges, seller personalities, and deal structures. I learned a lot in a relatively short amount of time—and I soon found that others were interested in what I'd learned as well. Throughout my acquisitions, countless friends and colleagues expressed curiosity about buying a business but admitted to not knowing where to start. I hadn't known either, so I wrote the book that I wish I'd had when I began.

This is not intuitive or common knowledge—most successful professionals are unfamiliar with the process of acquiring a business and may assume it is similar to other large purchases. It is natural to try to draw parallels with buying a home or an investment property—but in truth, it is a completely different experience. A rude realization awaits those who are not adequately prepared for the distinct stages of business acquisition, which can lead to significant delays and stress at best, and frustration and abandonment at worst.

This guide covers business acquisition from start to finish, with the chapters ordered chronologically to reflect the deal process. I've structured it such that you can refer to chapters individually, as standalone spot checks, if you are already familiar with some of the content. Acquiring a small or medium-sized business can seem complex, but this book is designed to steer you through the process step by step. It walks you through the most common deal structures, highlights key milestones, and flags potential pitfalls at each stage. To bring these ideas to life, I've interspersed a few personal anecdotes that provide real-world illustrations of the concepts described.

The content is presented in a plain-language, high-level manner because I want to make this large and complex undertaking understandable and accessible to everyone. For those with less business experience, finance terms are broken down into simple, easy-to-understand definitions, with important concepts highlighted **in bold** for quick reference.

The advice herein is targeted at first-time buyers without an MBA or finance/investing background and aims to make the journey as straightforward and approachable as possible. It is not intended as a be-all and end-all guide to M&A but rather as an introduction for potential first-time business buyers interested in pursuing ETA. To be clear, formal business training helps, and professional advisors will always be necessary, but this book can serve as a baseline introduction to set you up for success.

For my fellow mid-careerists, you have honed your business skills in the real world and, depending on your level of exposure to the intricacies of business operations and financial terms, the advice herein can range from too basic to too advanced. Likewise, the concepts in this guide may be more or less relevant to your needs, depending on your chosen industry and deal structure. I encourage you to seek out the information that is of value to you, knowing that some details may be redundant in light of your existing knowledge base.

Before we jump in, a word of caution: If you are intrigued but also concerned with the risk involved, you are doing it right. You *should* be uneasy about taking the life-changing step of buying a company, and your pursuit of the best fit should be soberly and prayerfully contemplated. It is a long-term decision, requiring a multiyear commitment, and there are sure to be seasons of intense stress—and even a desire to return to the comfort of punching a clock.

Perhaps even more unsettling is the prospect of financial risk and career derailment, especially if you are a mid-careerist who has enjoyed a decade or two of predictable W-2 salaries. The weight of the decision becomes heavier with an increasing number of dependents and obligations: A spouse, children, mortgage, and student debt make the golden handcuffs tighter. Simply put, you have more to lose with each passing day, so the best time to start is *now*—but that requires leaving behind the comfortable and familiar rhythm you have settled into. You will never be younger or have a longer career runway than you do today!

Yes, there will be moments of discomfort and unease, but the drawbacks are outweighed by the potential upsides of business ownership, not only in terms of wealth creation but also in terms of potential impact on your customers and community. So, what are you waiting for? Reflect on what may be causing you to hesitate: Do you lack a basic understanding of the terms and structure involved in businesses? Are you overwhelmed by the unfamiliar and lengthy process? Do you struggle to determine how much risk you would be assuming? Are you simply uncertain about where to start? This book is meant to help. Kudos to you for taking action!

CHAPTER 1

WHY TO BUY A SMALL BUSINESS

"Take this job and shove it; I ain't working here no more."[2]

—"Take This Job and Shove It," lyrics by David Allan Coe, performed by Johnny Paycheck

If you're a mid-careerist, you have likely been in the workforce for ten to twenty years, holding two to three different roles, probably with some level of supervisory or management responsibility. At this stage, you may have a little extra money put aside and, as your kids have gotten older, you now have a bit more time on your hands. We can all agree that the scenario of having disposable income plus the free time to spend it is ideal—but that equation doesn't necessarily add up to fulfillment. You might be asking yourself, "Why do I feel restless and dissatisfied—or even miserable—in my job?"

2 David Allan Coe, "Take This Job and Shove It," performed by Johnny Paycheck, Epic Records, 1977.

The answer is often your lack of autonomy in decision-making and the inability to see a direct correlation between your input (work hours, stress, unrequited loyalty) and output (compensation, time off, authority, mission). This discontent is what has brought you to your own crossroads: Something has to change—which means *you* must do something different.

For me, doing something different meant leaving the corporate world behind. I knew I should be grateful for the many opportunities in front of me, but none of them felt quite right. The roles that mirrored my experiences felt like just another verse of the same familiar song, and the ones that were further outside my comfort zone left me questioning whether I was truly excited about the work itself or just drawn to the novelty of something different. The idea of launching my own—or even leading someone else's—start-up had its appeal, but the weight of uncertainty gnawed at me. Was taking such a big risk bold and visionary, or just selfish and irresponsible if things didn't pan out? I felt stuck—torn between returning to a large organization, with its large and predictable problems, or leaping into the unknown with a high-risk start-up.

It wasn't until I discovered entrepreneurship through acquisition (ETA) that everything clicked. Here was a path that offered the best of both worlds, providing the autonomy to build something meaningful within the stability of an established business—and with the potential for real financial upside.

Reasons to Buy a Small Business

With discretionary time and financial resources, you could start your own business, invest in real estate or the stock market, or find a side hustle. While these are each strong options in their own right, they do not solve the problem of relying on a dissatisfying job to make ends meet. And while buying real estate or publicly traded securities can be lucrative over time, you have little to no influence on the outcome of your invested capital. So, can you pursue fulfilling work while making a good investment that you have control over? Yes—by buying a small business.

You do not have to conjure up a novel idea, develop a new product, or start a business from scratch in order to be an entrepreneur—that is the core tenet of ETA. This is where you, as a natural-born entrepreneur, can skip to the front of the line. Find a company that is doing it right, and use its day-one profits to customize and accelerate your own vision. Let's look at the major reasons to do so.

IT GIVES YOU GREATER AUTONOMY THAN ANY JOB EVER WILL

Owning a business provides the autonomy to create value on your own terms. Freedom to direct one's own path is likely the top reason motivating acquisition entrepreneurs. Small business ownership automatically makes you the boss, and as the boss, you control how you spend your time and how much you get paid. You are free from the hierarchical management structures, the corporate approvals, and parent office decisions that slowly crush your soul. The agency afforded by business ownership allows you to direct your efforts to the tasks and causes that matter to you instead of climbing the ranks in someone else's company.

Likewise, there is a direct and linear, if not potentially exponential, relationship between the energy and effective decision-making you pour into the business and the outcomes you achieve, including your own compensation. And if you do not like the direction the business is going, you can pivot. Small business ownership allows you to build the environment that you and your employees want to work in.

In addition to the freedom to choose where to direct your attention, the other primary reason to pursue small business ownership is wealth creation for you and your family. Owning and growing a successful business is foundational to the American Dream. Of note, while *wealth* can be synonymous with financial gain, the meaning of the word is actually much broader. As exemplified by one of my favorite sayings—the rich have money, and the wealthy have time. In addition to financial value, owning a business allows you to pursue your passion, determine your own schedule, and align your company's mission with a purpose that you find meaningful.

IT'S MORE EFFICIENT AND RELIABLE THAN STARTING FROM SCRATCH

Whether you are looking for long-term stability or a shorter-term hold for scaling and exiting, buying an already profitable business is a quicker and more reliable path than launching a start-up. Conventional wisdom says that if something is going to be decidedly *yours*, you must start it from scratch, right? News headlines are filled with exciting stories of the average guy who turned an idea into a billion-dollar company, so-called unicorns. While the headlines are inspiring, these rags-to-riches tales often glaze over the harsh realities of the start-up world: Most start-ups fail, and the ones that succeed commonly endure years of negative returns, product and strategy pivots, and employee churn.

Building a start-up is *hard*, and many shutter before they can get traction. Conservatively, it takes a start-up at least two to three years before generating predictable profits. According to *Harvard Business Review*, more than two-thirds of start-ups never deliver a positive return to investors.[3] There are many reasons that start-ups struggle to succeed, including the two biggest ones, which underpin nearly 70 percent of failures: lack of product–market fit and running out of money.[4]

If there is so much doom and gloom in the start-up world, why is venture capital (VC) investing so hyped? The typical VC firm spreads its risk over several start-ups, knowing that most will flop but hoping for a couple of big winners in the group to subsidize the fund's overall returns. At best, in a portfolio of ten venture-backed start-ups, three to four will fail, another three to four will return investors' capital around breakeven, and two to three will produce outsized returns.[5]

If you can tolerate the uncertainty and have the time, money, and energy to bring your idea to life for the benefit of all mankind, then do it! No doubt, you can have some *really* big wins, and I am a huge fan of those who see a need and tackle a problem with an innovative solution. But you do not have to be a founder to be an entrepreneur.

Many of us choose the entrepreneurial route of buying an established and profitable business as a faster and lower-risk path—a more reliable means of both leaving our mark on the world and creating wealth for our families. The predictable profits of an established business offer a comfortable measure of sustainability, as well as a built-in mechanism to support growth, instead of relying solely on outside capital.

---

3 Tom Eisenmann, "Why Start-Ups Fail: It's Not Always the Horse or the Jockey," *Harvard Business Review*, May–June 2021, https://hbr.org/2021/05/why-start-ups-fail.

4 "The Top 12 Reasons Startups Fail," CB Insights, August 3, 2021, https://www.cbinsights.com/research/startup-failure-reasons-top/.

5 Deborah Gage, "The Venture Capital Secret: 3 Out of 4 Start-Ups Fail," *The Wall Street Journal*, updated September 20, 2012, https://www.wsj.com/articles/SB10000872396390443720204578004980476429190.

THERE ARE MANY BUSINESS OWNERS LOOKING TO SELL

The gray wave of retirement is creating acquisition opportunities as business owners without a succession plan enter their golden years. A prime prospect for acquiring a company is an owner who has cultivated a mature and meaningful operation but has not identified a family member, business partner, or long-time employee to take ownership and sustain the business. Almost universally, these owners want their hard work and reputable name to live on, and you could be perfectly suited to help carry on their legacy and preserve their community standing by buying and running their company.

Luckily for you, the swell of retiring baby boomers (those born between 1946 and 1964) creates a large swath of companies from which to choose. *Forbes* estimates that half of all small businesses in America have owners who are fifty-five and older, and when these owners want to step away but do not have a succession plan, many of these companies will come on the market through the 2030s.[6] And it's not only baby boomers who are flooding the market with businesses to buy. In addition to retirement, other major changes to life circumstances, such as divorce or serious illness, can drive owners to want to sell.

For the seller, the desire to continue their legacy is often just as important as the money. The seller will be looking to see themselves in you and will want to know they can trust you with their baby. They want to be reassured that you will not come in and fire or severely disrupt their employees, some of whom are longtime personal friends. As a potential buyer, you can reassure them by sharing your vision of preservation and growth for their company.

---

6 Sardor Umrdinov, "Is Buying Boomer Businesses Now a Smart Move?", *Forbes*, August 4, 2023, https://www.forbes.com/sites/forbesbusinesscouncil/2023/08/04/is-buying-boomer-businesses-now-a-smart-move/.

THESE COMPANIES OFTEN PRESENT OPPORTUNITIES FOR GROWTH

From the investment side, owner-operated businesses can be some of the most stable and efficient companies, often including a tenured workforce with years of organizational knowledge. The other side of that coin is that these long-running family businesses can be sorely lacking in innovative and modernized processes; likewise, smaller companies may still be loosely managed and without formal structures commonly found in larger organizations, such as customer relationship management (CRM) systems or standardized human resources (HR) procedures. These unmanaged and/or outdated practices are juicy, ripe pieces of low-hanging fruit and offer high-impact opportunities to grow the business with minimal investment.

With a little patience and elbow grease, these operations can readily be professionalized and scaled. Streamlining systems and reducing variation helps the business work more efficiently, allowing it to produce more without increasing costs. This step alone could effectively increase your profitability and your exit multiple by a half (0.5×) or even a full (1×) turn of **earnings before interest, taxes, depreciation, and amortization (EBITDA)**—an important metric of financial performance, which we will elaborate on in the next chapter. By *exit*, I mean the point at which you, the owner or investor, cash out by selling the business or your ownership stake. If you want a path to a sizeable exit, remember, all big businesses once started out small.

OWNERSHIP DRIVES IMPACT AT THE COMMUNITY LEVEL

Small businesses are the cornerstone of the American economy, supporting the livelihoods of their employees and the surrounding communities. A 2019 report from the Small Business Administration (SBA) shows that small businesses (defined as having five hundred or fewer employees) drive 44 percent of economic activity in the United States.[7] More importantly, small businesses support local economies by creating sustainable jobs and propelling community growth and innovation. Additionally, business ownership allows women and minorities a ready path to achieving financial independence, especially in environments where other opportunities may be limited.

Recognizing the critical role of small businesses in the economy, the US government, through the SBA, offers tailored support to acquisition entrepreneurs through programs such as the SBA 7(a) loan. Often simply called an SBA loan, this program incentivizes investment in small businesses by providing accessible financing options not otherwise found through traditional avenues. I'll explain the pros and cons in greater detail in chapter 7, which discusses different types of funding.

Community impact is an important benefit of owning a small business, and it is especially meaningful when the investment is in a place that has sentimental value to you. Societal impact is hardly ever the sole reason to do a deal, but it is a rewarding positive nonetheless. By buying and continuing to operate a business that may have otherwise closed its doors, you keep mothers and fathers and teenagers in jobs that provide for their needs. When you are able to prevent employees and customers from having to leave your community, the economic stability of the region grows. The same investment amount that would be insignificant as a limited partner in an institutional fund or in commercial real estate can have a noticeable impact in a smaller community—say, by reopening a shuttered retirement home,

7 Jason Doré, "Small Businesses Generate 44 Percent of U.S. Economic Activity," US Small Business Administration Office of Advocacy, January 30, 2019, https://advocacy.sba.gov/2019/01/30/small-businesses-generate-44-percent-of-u-s-economic-activity/.

taking over a small manufacturing site, or buying and expanding a busy daycare. For many, this can be the key to regaining the feeling of impact and purpose that is often lacking in a corporate career.

My most meaningful investment to date has been acquiring a beloved senior living facility in my hometown of Trenton, Tennessee, through a partnership with longtime family friends. For me, the facility holds years of youthful memories of visiting the residents there through Girl Scouts service projects and church youth group holiday programs. After the acquisition, my partners and I invested in fully renovating the retirement community, returning it to the popular status it enjoyed after first opening in the 1950s. It now provides a safe and active independent living environment for local seniors—including some who are parents of my childhood friends and others who were once my teachers. Even better, the residents there are making their own collective contributions to the community through interactions with the local high school and nonprofit organizations.

Why Not to Buy a Small Business

Buying a small business is a terrific option for some people, but it's not for everyone. If you are curious about whether it's the right choice for you and intrigued by the prospect of being a small business owner, dedicating some discretionary time, energy, and resources to exploring acquisition entrepreneurship is a reasonable way to dip your toe in the water. But let me be clear: Buying a business is almost certainly the largest investment you will ever make. It is a massive responsibility that could jeopardize your family's financial future and put the livelihoods of dozens, if not hundreds, of other people at stake.

Please take the time to evaluate why this path is appealing to you, to ensure you are not simply trying to buy another job. One of the best pieces of advice I ever got about switching career paths came from my longtime executive coach at a point when I knew I wanted to do something different but wasn't sure what. He told me, "Make sure you are running toward something, not just away from something else." To assess that critical nuance, ask yourself the following questions.

CAN YOU THRIVE WITHOUT GUARDRAILS?

Do you thrive in setting a vision, mapping out the steps from here to there, and structuring your day to accomplish the most important tasks? Being a small business owner will require initiative and task prioritization on the daily, not only for yourself but also for your employees. It is appealing to think about being the boss and not having anyone tell you what to do, but remember that the pendulum swings both ways: Not only will you have to structure your own time, but you will also be direction-setting for everyone else in the company, delineating tasks and timelines for your direct reports. If you can see the vision in your head and enjoy setting the journey's course, then you will find freedom and satisfaction in choosing your own adventure. However, many people, including tenured executives, find this level of independence unsettling because it precipitates a feeling of being rudderless. Although they had not realized it, they formerly enjoyed being given a clear direction on what to do and a set deadline for completion.

ARE YOU READY TO BE THE CHIEF PROBLEM-SOLVER?

Throughout my career, I cannot think of anything more irritating than hearing someone at work say, "That's not my job." If you have ever uttered those words, first go apologize to your old boss—and then promptly remove this phrase from your vocabulary. Permanently. When you are a small business owner, *everything* is your job. All problems are your problems, and the buck stops with you. In fact, you will get all of the hardest problems, because the easier ones got solved before making it to your level. And hard problems are usually on the gray scale, because the easy ones are black and white. You must make judgment calls, often without a full fact pattern or complete dataset—and there is sometimes a lot at stake, such as the future of the company. If you are one of these folks who has all the answers, then being the chief problem-solver might be alluring to you, but check yourself against a concept I learned at US Army War College (I attended one of their civilian programs in 2022): If you have a quick answer for a big problem, you don't know all the details and/or you aren't responsible for the outcomes. Being an armchair quarterback is just not the same as having to make the final call.

DO YOU HAVE THE FINANCIAL FREEDOM TO COMFORTABLY TAKE THIS PATH?

Are you dependent on a steady and predictable salary that hits your bank account on a regular schedule? There should rarely, if ever, be an issue in making payroll because you are going to acquire an enduringly profitable company with recurring revenue and foreseeable costs. Still, crises pop up and unexpected opportunities arise that require you to deploy all available cash, and that could even mean your own paycheck. Small business ownership is not for the faint of heart! You must be able to tolerate dramatic ups and downs and weather the storm of financial instability, all the while acting as a shock absorber for your employees.

ARE YOU PREPARED TO BE "ON THE CLOCK" TWENTY-FOUR SEVEN?

Owning a business, especially one that is stable and well run, allows you the autonomy and freedom to spend your time as you see fit. You do not even have to be on-site every day—in fact, you probably should not hover over managers and employees but instead give them the leeway to execute your vision within your parameters. You will remember from your own days of being an employee that being micro-managed and watched constantly is both annoying and unproductive. With that said, having the flexibility to come and go as desired is not a license to be an absentee boss. Small business ownership is much more than a job. It is 24/7/365, including Christmas Eve, Sunday afternoons, and during your European vacation. Because you are the chief problem-solver, and because problems do not always pop up during weekday work hours, it means you are always on the clock.

You Think ETA Might Be Right for You–What Now?

I hope this has resonated with you as a balanced approach. There are several benefits to small business ownership, as it allows you to pave your own path to executing a vision and building wealth. Likewise, there are a handful of sticky wickets to consider. Without some introspection, you might be tempted to pursue the wrong path. After a clearheaded evaluation, if you are still interested in ETA, you've already won the battle of the heart—you have the fire in your belly to do this. Now, it's time for the battle of the mind, making sure you are logically pursuing a smart path. Toward that end, let's look at the qualities that make for a good acquisition.

CHAPTER 2

WHAT AM I LOOKING FOR?

***"It's far better to buy a wonderful company at a fair price than a fair company at a wonderful price."*[8]**

—*Warren Buffett*

I will apologize in advance for the cliché, but it does ring true here: If you don't know what you're looking for, you won't know when you've found it. Having a clear picture of your ideal acquisition target is easy for some entrepreneurs, and it may even already have a name and an address. However, for many, the image of what a great opportunity looks like is fuzzier. You may be attracted to a concept or have a general idea of where you want to land, but that's it.

For my traditional search fund acquisition, I was sure about two things: I knew the financial sweet spot my institutional sponsor preferred ($1 million–$5 million in EBITDA), and I knew I wanted to stay within driving distance of Nashville. And since healthcare is all I know, sticking to that industry was a no-brainer. But within healthcare, there

---

8 Warren E. Buffett, *Berkshire Hathaway Inc. Shareholder Letter - 1989* (Omaha, NE: Berkshire Hathaway Inc., 1990), https://www.berkshirehathaway.com/letters/1989.html.

are endless verticals, and I struggled to define my focus without making it too narrow. I considered the "hot" sectors at the time—businesses such as aesthetic practices, dental roll-ups, and infusion centers—but I knew I'd be competing with big private equity (PE) funds and likely overpaying. On the other end of the spectrum, there were the tried-and-true models, such as primary care practices and home-based services, which are stable but tough to scale profitably.

In the end, I took a different approach—defining the characteristics I wanted in a business first and then filtering potential companies through that lens. I knew I wanted something scalable through technology (no brick-and-mortar physician practices) and aligned with my mission to serve rural and underserved populations (so a med spa was out). If you'd asked me at the start whether I was looking for a mail-order specialty pharmacy, I would've said, "No way," but it ended up being the perfect fit. I've seen many searchers struggle because they defined their focus too narrowly or too rigidly, and I was determined not to make that mistake. Now I want to help you avoid that error as well. A good starting point: developing your search thesis.

Develop Your Search Thesis

Whether you already have something in mind and want to confirm you are on the right path or you need help defining the kind of target that will best suit your needs, the best place to begin is to outline your deal criteria by developing a **search thesis**. Yes, even individual acquisition entrepreneurs need a thesis—they are not just for institutional investors. Of note, when you are both the searcher and the investor, the terms *search thesis* and *investment thesis* are often used interchangeably.

You can make your thesis as simple or robust as you want, but the more specific you are, the easier and quicker it will be to rule out companies that are not a fit. In addition to using this as your own lens in evaluating companies, your search thesis will be key to conveying your priorities to investors and lenders when describing why your target is attractive and worthy of their financing.

In his article, "Smart Shopping for Businesses: A Guide to Acquiring Diamonds, Not Dust," Roland Frasier likens setting acquisition criteria to buying products online.[9] You do not scroll endlessly, hoping you'll stumble on something you like. Rather, you use filters and search terms to drill down to what you want. The filters in your search become your investment criteria, which are strung together in a search thesis. Whether or not you plan to use a formal search thesis statement in a pitch to investors, I think it is a useful exercise to define one so you can more objectively qualify targets. As an investor myself, I'm always drawn to those pursuing ETA who can clearly articulate what they're looking for, why it aligns with their strategy, and how their target fits the criteria. A well-defined focus not only demonstrates conviction but also signals a thoughtful and disciplined approach to evaluating opportunities.

At a minimum, your search thesis should contain components of your preferences for the following:

1. **Industry and business model:** In what space does your ideal company operate (retail, manufacturing, healthcare, etc.), and how does it interact in the marketplace (services or products)? Examples: pest control provider, retail consumer goods, water delivery service, healthcare revenue cycle support, software solutions supplier.

---

9 Roland Frasier, "Smart Shopping for Businesses: A Guide to Acquiring Diamonds, Not Dust," Roland Frasier's Newsletter, January 21, 2024, accessed March 26, 2025, https://roland.beehiiv.com/p/smart-shopping-businesses-guide-acquiring-diamonds-not-dust?utm_source=substack&utm_medium=email.

2. **Geography:** What is your preferred location, and how flexible are you? Examples: located in the Atlanta metro area, preferably in the Pacific Northwest, anywhere in the continental US with a large logistics hub (seaport/airport).
3. **Size:** How is the business's size defined financially or operationally? Examples: from $10 million–$30 million in annual revenue, a single (or multisite) operation, at least $1 million in EBITDA, no more than 250 employees.
4. **Mission:** What do you want this company to accomplish or provide in terms of the target audience, unique offering, or goal achieved? Examples: provides an eco-friendly energy source, expands opportunities for minority populations, offers online educational content.
5. **Opportunity for value creation:** What can you bring to the table to increase the value of the company? Examples: expand footprint into new markets, improve efficiency through technology, diversify product offerings.

After you have developed short phrases for each of these components, string them together, and voilà—you now have a basic search thesis! Not only will this rudimentary framing assist you in reviewing deals, but it will also serve as a short and memorable elevator pitch when telling others what you are looking for. Here are a few examples of memorable and specific investment theses:

I am searching for an established educational technology software platform with $5 million–$15 million annual recurring revenue with clients across the US, that offers innovative tools for online learning and student engagement and has the potential for state government and local school board contracts.

I am looking for a small metal fabrication shop in Texas that consistently has an annual profit of $500,000 or more, provides high-quality custom metal components for specific industries, and can build long-term relationships with niche clients requiring stringent production criteria.

I want to buy a sustainable farming operation in the Pacific Northwest with a purchase price under $2 million that enhances food security, minimizes environmental impact, and can grow through partnerships with eco-conscious retailers.

Going through this exercise may have highlighted the fact that you have not yet considered some of these key factors, or perhaps you have thought about them but are not sure exactly what you prefer. Once you have settled on your parameters, keep an open mind when applying criteria to potential targets and strive to do so without bias or preconceived ideas. Remember, if you do what you have always done, you know what you will get, so think outside the box. This is the time to explore ways to apply your expertise and experience in an adjacent—or perhaps even completely new—space.

Preliminary Due Diligence: Is It a Fit?

When you have identified a qualifying target, you will begin **preliminary due diligence**—the process of evaluating the company's suitability as a business investment. Is it the right size for you? Does it fit your skill set and personality? Has it performed well in the past, and does it have a bigger and brighter future ahead? Let's dig into each of these points to help focus on the best acquisition target for your unique situation. In this chapter, I'll explore the "fit factors"—is the business of appropriate scale, and is it a good match in terms of objectives, mission, values, etc.? The next chapter will focus on the practicalities of past financial performance and future promise.

The main goal of this preliminary due diligence phase when evaluating a potential target: *Get to "no" quickly.* As badly as you may want to find a business and settle a deal, the most important part of the process is weeding out poor choices fast. Not only does this discipline keep you focused on your intended target, it also speeds the overall acquisition process by covering the many rabbit holes down which you might be tempted to jump.

Additionally, setting criteria ahead of time helps keep emotions at bay. You might be surprised at how strongly you can get caught up in your feelings when pursuing a deal—say, because you really like the people, the product is innovative, or the location is ideal. You must not let those intangibles drive a bad investment. Just like buying a car or walking into a casino, it is imperative that you set parameters ahead of time and clearly know where your lines in the sand are drawn so your decisions are rational. Rule number one in acquisitions: Don't. Get. Attached. Instead of letting your feelings call the shots, focus on the following fit factors.

SIZE

While the right-size target will vary from person to person according to comfort level, experience, risk tolerance, and financing, there are some generally accepted criteria that make for a meaningful role now and a rewarding return at exit. The term *small business* is relative, especially given the SBA's wide-ranging definition: an enterprise with fewer than five hundred employees. If the term conjures mental images of your local hair salon or the neighborhood corner store, you would be right. While these types of "single shingle" businesses are the lifeblood of America, they are generally not a common investment target because of their tiny footprint and limited reach.

For the principles and processes covered in this guide, we will focus on **small and medium-sized businesses (SMBs)**, sometimes referred to as **small and medium-sized enterprises (SMEs)**. In investor parlance, these relatively larger small businesses fall into the category of the **lower middle market (LMM)**, broadly defined as companies with annual revenues of $5 million to $50 million. Clearly, these are not small or insignificant numbers. These "small" businesses are termed such because they are often specialized and niche.

LMM businesses comprise the largest number of businesses in the US economy, and businesses falling into this category are an increasingly popular target of not only strategic buyers but also investment firms.[10] What's all the fuss about? These targets offer acquirers more choices for growth potential and lower valuations. At first, you might worry that this heightened down-market attention will make for a more competitive environment. Fortunately for you, LMM PE funds are generally not interested in companies with EBITDA below $3 million because of their often-inefficient business models. Companies below this financial mark usually are not prepared to move quickly through a transaction and, postclosing, require too much hands-on intervention. These owner-operated businesses are better suited to acquisition entrepreneurs—like you!—and offer a unique opportunity to add value through brand professionalization, optimization of efficient workflows, and scalable structures.

But, how small is too small? As a first-time buyer, it is tempting to believe that microbusinesses are easier to acquire and simpler to operate, but this is often untrue. During an acquisition, businesses on the small end of the spectrum take the same amount of blood,

---

10 David Bickerton, "Lower Middle Market," *Wall Street Oasis*, last updated October 12, 2024, https://www.wallstreetoasis.com/resources/skills/valuation/lower-middle-market.

sweat, and tears as larger ones. In fact, smaller ones may take more time because of the lack of formality and organization of financial and operational documents. Likewise, these companies may not be represented by a sophisticated broker (or any broker at all) because of the limited size of the business or cost-consciousness on the seller's part. Often, the seller of a smaller business likely plays an active operational role, which can slow the diligence process and present a **key person risk**—meaning that too much of the business's success is wrapped up in one individual's efforts, expertise, or connections. In my experience, my smallest acquisition was my most difficult, and I doubt I'll ever do a sub–$1 million EBITDA deal again.

If you are a rookie buyer, and particularly if you are a first-time CEO, be wary of the trap of seeking comfort in a smaller business, assuming it to be more manageable and easier to understand. Hiring mistakes and strategic or operational missteps can happen to anyone, especially those who lack tenure in the captain's chair. These miscues eat up the company's precious cash flow, and the operational conundrum of smaller companies (such as certain employees filling multiple roles, leading to workarounds or shortcuts) makes it harder to identify the cause and effect of different business levers. Businesses that are a little further upmarket (larger) offer cushioning to absorb a first-time CEO's inevitable mistakes.

The right size business for you is going to be custom fit, driven by your operational and mission sweet spots. If you are accustomed to leading larger teams and can raise external capital, go bigger—you will have backing. Cast your net widely, guided by overarching principles and a defined financial range, not specifics. Especially if you are constrained geographically, meaning you cannot or will not move, be creative and think broadly, keeping in mind that online businesses generate cash and are not tied to a specific city or state.

EVENTUAL EXIT PLAN

While it seems too far into the future to contemplate, you must also choose your target's size with the eventual exit in mind. To attract interest from serious financial and strategic buyers, your business will need to have at least $10 million in revenue at the time of sale. Unless you're planning to hold the business long term, most small business buyers—and certainly their investors—will expect a **liquidity event** within five to eight years. A liquidity event is a transaction that allows investors to convert their equity into cash, typically through a partial or full sale to another entity. To maximize your exit multiple (more on that soon), the business's size at acquisition and its projected growth trajectory should support the financial outcome you're ultimately aiming for.

When considering future growth trajectory, you also want to ensure a small company has enough cash flow to fund your **value creation initiatives**—the improvements and expansions you want to make after acquisition. Otherwise, you risk being stagnant. And don't forget that small businesses often lack the technological infrastructure and business processes required to support scalability, so factor in the cost of these upgrades when assessing cash flow adequacy.

AFFORDABILITY

A discussion about the right size business to pursue should include not only what you prefer but also what you can afford. If you plan to finance the acquisition through your own funds or a personally guaranteed SBA 7(a) loan, your budget will be smaller than someone with an institutional sponsor or syndicate of investors and a prequalified commitment from a bank for the company's cash flow financing. At this point in preliminary due diligence, you will only need a general idea of your financial parameters. You can take some comfort in knowing that your offer—made through a **letter of intent (LOI)**, which outlines the preliminary agreement between both parties—is nonbinding and will include contingencies, such as securing financing.

PERSONAL GOALS

After determining your preferences on size and affordability, the next question you should seek to answer is, "Will I find fulfillment and joy in running this company for the next ten years?" Of all the factors to evaluate when pursuing an acquisition, finding the right fit is the most intangible and personal, requiring introspection and occasionally answering hard questions, even ones you may not have otherwise considered. Admittedly, this assessment is mostly subjective, but it should not be emotional or only a gut feeling. Be honest and frank with yourself when considering whether your intended target is best suited to your unique situation, and be quick to "phone a friend" familiar with your work style to mitigate any blind spots. Of course, more than any of the others, this important effort of ensuring the right fit should always include a detailed conversation with your spouse and/or close family members who know you best.

An acquisition target that's the right fit for you will not only be a strong business venture but will also bring meaning to your daily work. Clarifying what suits you best doesn't just help after the acquisition—it also increases your chances of standing out in a competitive process with other buyers. Articulating how acquiring a particular company meets your personal goals helps differentiate you from the sea of financial buyers and will demonstrate to the seller how you translate your passion into a vision for continuing their legacy.

GEOGRAPHY

Geography is another critical fit factor. Is the business in a location where you would like to live and work for the next several years? This is essentially a moot point with digital/online businesses, but for everything else, you need to be comfortable with moving there or easily commuting. This also includes consideration of your spouse's preferences, school choices, distance from extended family, etc. And, depending on the business, you should also consider the demographics and economic trajectory of the region, including the area's reputation for safety and its tourism potential, which could drive growth potential for your target. Likewise, geography is an important factor when determining the relative ease or difficulty of recruiting talent to the organization.

MISSION

Another fit-related consideration is whether or not the company aligns with your internal mission and desired career trajectory. Ask yourself, "What problem is this business solving, and do I care about that?" A purposeful connection between your personal and professional realms leads to a meaningful and satisfying life, and finding the right business can accelerate your personal growth while helping you achieve your desired impact in the world. For many of us, this takes the form of faith-based objectives, striving to transform our communities—and the people in them—into something better because of our work. There is plenty of satisfaction in creating jobs for others and a comfortable existence for yourself, with the ability to give back to the causes and people you love. In short, if you do not believe in the mission of your work, it will be just another job—but with more headaches, risk, and responsibility.

REQUIRED KNOWLEDGE AND SKILLS

Take a serious look at the skills and expertise required to be successful in this business and assess if your professional strengths and your network can be leveraged to grow the company. There is a fine line between stepping beyond your direct experience to try something a little different and entering exotic territory to pursue a challenge. A new(ish) take on a familiar trade is invigorating and creates the opportunity to flex your well-defined muscles in a fresh way. But beware of the steep learning curve associated with delving into a novel industry. Even with a seasoned management team surrounding you, true value creation and growth are enhanced when the vision-setter has a nuanced understanding of the business, its customers, and how it fits into the industry at large. If you are convinced that leaping into the unknown is the right choice for you, at least make sure the company you are pursuing has enough cushion to absorb the ramp-up time and newbie mistakes that you will inevitably make.

I personally believe that the business should be in an industry or service with which you have expertise and experience. Your accumulated knowledge of market dynamics, key players, and growth levers will accelerate your ability to build on the company's success and troubleshoot, or even predict, issues more effectively. You have spent years building a network in your field—why wouldn't you want to leverage it now, especially when the rewards of doing so come directly to you?

EMOTIONAL IMPACT

Finally, an important component that cannot be quantified, but is nonetheless relevant, is how the business makes you feel, which is a reflection of the target organization's culture. In addition to your objective assessment of the work and subject matter itself, you will also subjectively, as my teenagers say, "feel some kind of way" about the culture of the company. If every interaction gives you an icky feeling, your gut may be telling you something. A question here could be "Is your leadership style and philosophy a good fit for the organization's culture?" Given that organizational culture is difficult and slow to change, consider whether the employees' baseline attitudes and habits can likely be optimized with a little tweaking or if your strategy will be devoured for breakfast by a resistant, ingrained culture.

Success Is More Than Just the Numbers

Clearly, deciding whether a business is the right fit for you is an entirely specific and mostly subjective process, but a wise acquirer holds these intangible qualities in just as high regard as the black-and-white metrics of a business. Aligning your values and professional skill set with the right organizational fit lays the foundation for long-term success in your new company.

Of course, that's not to say that the tangibles—such as past profitability—are to be discounted. The next chapter dives deeper into the money-related elements of preliminary due diligence, touching specifically on how to assess past financial performance and predict future gains.

RN BO
TURAL-
BORN
RAL-N

CHAPTER 3

DIGGING DEEPER: HISTORICAL FINANCIALS AND FUTURE OUTLOOK

"The longer you can look back, the farther you can look forward."[11]

—*Winston Churchill*

In addition to the softer side of the analysis of a potential target, the real meat and potatoes of evaluating the health of a company is diving into its objective data. A strong financial track record, with an equally sturdy outlook, is an unmistakable key marker of an attractive acquisition target and one of the most important factors in your decision to purchase a company. There are entire books, degrees, and professions

11 "Quotes Falsely Attributed to Winston Churchill," International Churchill Society, January 17, 2023, https://winstonchurchill.org/resources/quotes/quotes-falsely-attributed/.

focused solely on this topic, so we will only scratch the surface here in order to familiarize you with how to initially vet options at a high level.

Even if you are comfortable reading an income statement, it is imperative that you engage a trained finance/accounting professional when considering acquiring a business. This should be an individual who has specific experience with business acquisitions. I have seen people using the same community certified public accountant (CPA) who does their taxes to try to do a business valuation/outlook, and I've seen sellers have the same attorney who wrote their will try to write a three hundred–plus page business purchase agreement. These endeavors rarely end well. Your financial future is too important to risk on the advice of your uncle who works in accounting or your golf buddy who sold his company.

If most of your career has been in the operations space, you may not be as familiar with the financial terms being thrown around in acquisition conversations. In which case, you have come to the right place! This book's intent is to guide first-time buyers who do not have a background in finance and to demystify the process for mid-careerists making the transition to business owners. Do not feel intimidated by these basic concepts: The core principles you need to know are not complicated mathematical formulas but rather logical—and usually intuitive—measures of business performance. Fluency in these general metrics will help you weed through your target options before investing the time and resources needed for professional due diligence.

Digging into a company's past can be a tedious and time-consuming process—and it *should* be. Keep in mind that, with a vision of the past, you'll be able to get a better sense of the company's potential future. You want to know what value the organization has created previously—and what value it's capable of generating down the line. Getting into the details of things such as the past financial performance, business model, and competitive landscape is the best way to help determine that potential. There are also some key elements of a business that can help determine its capacity for future value creation, which we'll touch on as well. Ultimately, the value you create—by growing the business and increasing its worth—translates directly into wealth for you and your family when it's time to sell.

Past Financial Performance

First things first—the company you acquire should be making money legally and compliantly. While this obvious advice can provoke an expected eyeroll, it should be explicitly contemplated before moving forward. Confirm that the way the company is making money is legal and adheres to all applicable state and federal laws. In many instances, this will be a nonissue, but in more regulated industries, you may need to do some homework and potentially retain the services of an experienced advisor. There will be an opportunity to do a deeper dive into the financial integrity of the business later in the process, through the **quality of earnings (QoE)** assessment—a formal, audit-like analysis that evaluates the sustainability of revenue streams, expense trends, and accounting practices—but any acquisition target worth your time should immediately pass the smell test of above-board revenue generation.

Your initial assessment of the financial health of a business should incorporate at least three key considerations: profitability, efficiency, and liquidity. These indicators can be reasonably evaluated by reviewing the company's **balance sheet**, **income statement**, and **cash flow statement**, all of which should be readily available in the early stages of preliminary due diligence. Before we dig into the specific metrics you will want to review, let's break down the overarching purpose of each of these report cards:

- **Balance sheet:** This is a point-in-time snapshot of what the business owns (assets) and what it owes (liabilities). This overview is used to determine shareholder equity, which is essentially the net worth of the business to its owners.
- **Income statement:** This is a detailed account of the business's revenue, expenses, gains, and losses for a certain period of time (month or year). Also known as a **profit and loss statement,** its insights reveal the company's financial performance and operational efficiency over time and provide a picture of trends in revenue and expenses across longer time frames.
- **Cash flow statement:** This is a financial statement that details the cash moving in and out of the business from the three primary areas of operations, investments, and financing. Measured over a certain time period, the picture of cash inflows and outflows helps gauge the company's performance in both generating and managing cash.

Ideally, you will want to look at each of these statements from a historical perspective, generally for the last five years, to identify trends and compare performance over time. This retrospective overview is particularly important if an extraordinary event occurred in the company during the last few years; this could be an internal circumstance, such as the divestiture of a division or move of a facility, or an external force, such as a pandemic or supply chain disruption. Use caution when interpreting the significance of a one-time occurrence, as sellers tend to over- or under-ascribe the impact of the event on the company's performance. Reviewing the financials for several periods both before and after the extraordinary event can offset the seller's attempts to use it as a catch-all for explaining away ongoing underlying issues.

Another note of warning when reviewing financial statements is the leeway sometimes taken in forecasting the company's financial performance into the future. During the preliminary due diligence phase, you will likely be presented with a **pro forma income statement**, which predicts expected revenue and expenses going forward several quarters or years into the future. When included as part of a sale process, these projections can be inflated to drive the company's valuation and, consequently, purchase price. Approach these projections with caution, particularly noting if year-over-year revenue growth is consistent with prior performance and ensuring that appropriate assumptions are baked in for the natural rise in expenses, especially labor costs. Use what you know about the business to make your own conservative predictions for the next few years and then compare notes with the seller on any material discrepancies.

Using these standard statements to focus on the three key markers of financial performance—profitability, efficiency, and liquidity—you should be able to succinctly explain to investors, lenders, and yourself how healthy the company has been over the past three to five years and, from there, determine what you can reasonably expect in the coming years, given similar conditions.

PROFITABILITY

Certainly, one of the first and most logical indicators of an attractive acquisition target is the company's **profitability**, which in its most basic form is measured by **net profit**, the money left over after all expenses have been subtracted from revenue. You will also want to calculate the **profit margin**, which is the portion of revenue that the company keeps as profit after accounting for all costs. Because this metric is expressed as a percentage, it can be used in a side-by-side comparison of businesses of different sizes or even industries. While there are a handful of profit margin calculations (gross profit margin, operating profit margin, EBITDA margin), the most telling marker of a company's financial health is its **net profit margin**, often simply called profit margin.

A company's net profit margin is calculated by subtracting all expenses, including interest and taxes, from operating income and then expressing that number as a percentage of revenue. Here is the formula, including how to calculate the components needed for the equation:

$$\frac{\text{(Operating Income - Other Expenses - Interest - Taxes)}}{\text{Revenue}} \times 100$$

Operating Income = Gross Profit - Operating Expenses
Gross Profit = Revenue - Cost of Goods Sold

Figure 3.1: The formula for net profit margin.

You can also calculate the **gross profit margin** from these numbers by dividing gross profit by revenue. The **cost of goods sold (COGS)** refers to the direct costs associated with producing or procuring products to sell. In the instance of a manufactured product, COGS includes raw materials and labor costs from production, but most of the time, the cost of labor is considered an operating expense. **Operating expenses** encompass all costs associated with running the business, including payroll, overhead (rent, utilities, insurance), sales and marketing, office supplies, and accounting and legal fees. The category *other expenses* in the net profit margin calculation is generally from the gain or loss from a one-time event, such as a legal settlement or an asset write-off. Interest (from a loan) and taxes are self-explanatory.

Let's say you are looking to buy a retail boutique that sells women's clothing and accessories. The company generates revenue through the sale of inventory procured from distributors and wholesalers, and the business has both brick-and-mortar and online storefronts. In order to determine the profitability of this boutique, you should calculate the net profit margin, which can be used to compare this business to a similar one in another town or, more broadly, to compare this retail business to a services business, for example.

Here is a high-level overview of key financial metrics found on the income statement:

In-store Sales	**$980,000**	
Online Sales	**+ $470,000**	
Total Revenue	**$1,450,000**	
Cost of Goods Sold	**- $580,000**	
Gross Profit	**$870,000**	
Gross Profit Margin	**60%**	**($870,000 ÷ $1,450,000) × 100**
Operating Expenses*	**- $350,000**	
Operating Income	**$520,000**	
Taxes	**- $120,000**	
Net Income	**$400,000**	
Net Profit Margin	**27.6%**	**($400,000 ÷ $1,450,000) × 100**

* *In our hypothetical boutique, primary operating expenses include payroll/benefits, advertising, shipping, and rent. There are no other expenses or interest payments incurred by the business.*

Figure 3.2: An example of how to calculate the net profit margin using key financial metrics.

Not only does this assessment give you a look at how much money can be made from business activities, it also indicates where you might find opportunities for value creation after acquisition. In our example, the net profit margin can be enhanced by increasing revenue through selling more products and/or raising prices, reducing labor costs by increasing online sales, or negotiating lower shipping costs through a logistics provider.

But wait, how can businesses of different sizes and varying capital structures be compared in a like-for-like manner? Through the all-powerful **EBITDA** metric and the related **EBITDA margin**. EBITDA (pronounced "EE-bit-dah") is probably the most well-regarded and frequently utilized financial performance indicator in acquisitions. The EBITDA calculation removes the noise of external capital, accounting factors, and tax burdens to give a more accurate indication of operational efficiency and potential profitability. In other words, it removes aspects that can be specific to a company, such as how much debt it carries or how much it pays in taxes, and gets down to the true financial picture.

EBITDA can be used to compare business performance across industries, regions, and sizes, and is calculated by adding the noncash expenses, such as **depreciation** (the amount of an asset's value lost over time, based on an accounting formula) and **amortization** (the amount of debt payment per the loan repayment schedule), to operating income. An even better metric to compare the profitability of different companies is a side-by-side assessment of each company's **EBITDA margin**, which is a profitability ratio that measures the percentage of a company's revenue that is left over after paying operating expenses.

Here are the formulas:

EBITDA = Revenue - COGS - Operating Expenses
(Excluding Depreciation and Amortization)

EBITDA Margin = (EBITDA ÷ Total Revenue) × 100

Using our hypothetical boutique example, here are the EBITDA and EBITDA margin calculations:

EBITDA = $1,450,000 - $580,000 - $350,000 = $520,000*
***If there is no depreciation or amortization, EBITDA = Operating Income**

EBITDA Margin = ($520,000 ÷ $1,450,000) × 100 = 35.9%

Figure 3.3: How to calculate EBITDA and EBITDA Margin.

One last note on EBITDA that is well known to brokers, bankers, and finance bros: EBITDA can be manipulated and/or sometimes paint a false picture if you do not know the right questions to ask. While it can be a useful metric, EBITDA alone doesn't always tell the whole story. First, it leaves out interest expenses, which can hide how much debt a business is carrying. Second, it excludes depreciation and amortization, which means the cost of maintaining or replacing assets might not be obvious. Third, sellers often present an **adjusted EBITDA**, which includes **addbacks**—expenses that are added back to EBITDA to reflect a clearer view of the business's recurring earnings. These often include one-time costs, owner compensation, or personal expenses that won't carry over to a new owner. Addbacks are common and often appropriate, but you have to evaluate whether they're legitimate exclusions or just padding to make the business look more profitable than it is. So, the key isn't just looking at EBITDA—it's knowing how to ask about what's behind the numbers.

EFFICIENCY

When looking at levers you can pull to add value, what you are really doing is evaluating the company's efficiency, specifically, its operational efficiency or the way it controls cost and uses resources. By reviewing the financial statements and asking a few key questions of the seller, an overview of the business's day-to-day operational efficiency can be done quickly, according to the time and resources required to deliver its services or produce its goods.

One clear marker is the company's cost efficiency. Are the production costs, operational expenses, and overhead used in line with industry benchmarks? In a cost-efficient business, the quality, output, and speed of production increase as costs decrease. A good measurement of this is inventory turnover, which allows the business to generate cash to pay its bills. Because a business cannot keep an unlimited supply of products, its **inventory turnover rate** is the speed at which a company moves merchandise through the business and to its customers. In general, a high inventory turnover rate is favorable, indicating prompt sales. However, the Goldilocks principle applies, as an inventory turnover rate that is *too* fast could mean the company struggles to keep up with customer demand, either from disorganized ordering or a stressed supply chain. Rather than too fast or too slow, the inventory turnover rate needs to be just right.

Another helpful way to gauge efficiency and identify potential opportunities for improvement after acquisition is to identify obvious sources of waste. Because you will only be provided with high-level information, this may be difficult to do in detail when initially evaluating a target, but careless expenditures that jump off the page can signal an immediate red flag. Common sources of waste in businesses include time and material waste from downtime or poorly designed processes, quality waste due to high rates of defects or required reworking, financial waste because of unnecessary overhead or excessive fees, and customer retention waste attributable to mediocre customer service and high customer turnover.

Finally, consider how the business is using its most valuable, and likely most expensive, resource—its employees. In almost every business, employee productivity can be approximated by measuring output per employee, whether that is in widgets produced, revenue generated, or services provided. In mature companies, comparing productivity over time or benchmarking output against industry norms can provide insights into current operations and potential improvements after acquisition. And because many small, family-owned businesses have lagged in implementing technology, you might also find areas of the business that could be automated partially or entirely through modernizing systems, or even just by turning on functionalities that already exist within the company's current software.

LIQUIDITY

Another noteworthy metric is capital efficiency, which is how effectively a business converts its investments into profits. This concept is known as **liquidity**, or the ease by which assets or inventory are converted to cash without taking a significant haircut on market value. Cash is the most liquid of all assets, because it can be quickly and easily converted into any other asset (inventory, supplies, equipment, etc.) While several ratios of liquidity can be calculated from the company's balance sheet, you, as a prospective buyer, will want to at least evaluate the business's financial efficiency through its cash conversion cycle, as well as its capital efficiency based on how it spends its money to operate and grow.

The financial efficiency of the business is tantamount to all other metrics discussed here. When a company successfully turns its expenses into revenue, it is stable and capable of sustainable growth. There are multiple ways to measure financial efficiency, all of which should be considered in total. A good place to start is assessing the **accounts receivable (AR) turnover ratio**. This metric does not apply to businesses that sell retail goods and require payment on the spot, but many service-related companies and distributors provide goods and services to customers and then send invoices for payment, which they must then wait patiently to receive. If customers pay their debts quickly, the company's AR turnover ratio is high, meaning it can collect what it is owed efficiently, resulting in a low number of **days in AR**, or the average number of days that pass between the sale and the payment collection.

A low turnover ratio in AR could indicate a deficient process for billing and collections, excessively lenient credit terms, or possibly even a customer base with financial difficulties. Ultimately, you want to look at the company's AR turnover trends over time and compare them to industry standards. Ideally, the company will have robust payment collection processes that have improved over time and outperform similar businesses. The AR turnover ratio is an important part of the entire **cash conversion cycle**, but it is just one step in a larger series of processes that account for the overall time, usually measured in days, that it takes the company to turn inventory into cash—in short, how long you must wait to see a dollar of profit made from a dollar spent.

Evaluating a business's objective metrics provides a crucial look into its operational efficiency, financial health, and current market position. Cutting through the flowery language and favorable spin that a seller might use, the data provides the proof in the pudding. While not a guarantee of future results, the company's past performance provides a basis for identifying both strengths and opportunities for improvement. This track record, when assessed in the context of its business model and market position, can gauge the company's ability to adapt and grow in the changing and unknown circumstances of tomorrow.

Assessing Future Trajectory

As we have seen in the last few sections, the smartest acquirers examine a business by looking into the rearview mirror at a company's history, as well as closely looking in their own mirror to gauge what is best for them personally. But even the most attractive mirror image will turn ugly unless the business is structured and positioned for optimal industry growth and is able to thrive with the value that you, as its new owner/operator, can create.

Predicting a company's future performance requires a keen inspection of its business model, market positioning, and opportunities for value creation. This assessment can help bring your crystal ball into clearer focus but will necessitate some market research on your part. This step is a worthwhile exercise, even for industry insiders, and is especially important if your target company does not fit squarely within the realm of your previous professional experience. Common sources of up-to-date industry news are trade publications, academic journals, consulting firms' white papers, financial and business websites, and market research databases. And you should certainly leverage another fountain of knowledge—subject matter experts within your own personal network.

The assessment of your target's business model, particularly ensuring that it is resilient and balanced, forms the foundation of this analysis. Such a model ensures that a company can grow nimbly and quickly, as well as withstand unpredictable events, such as a natural disaster or economic recession, thus maintaining stability even in tumultuous times. Evaluating how a company is positioned within its market helps refine this prediction by identifying growth levers as well as expected headwinds.

Last, the ability to recognize and seize opportunities for value creation underscores your target's potential for future success and, ultimately, the return on your investment of time and capital. This involves pinpointing unique ways that you, as the new owner, can bring added value to the company's offerings or operations, distinguishing itself from competitors and meeting emerging market demands effectively. Together, these elements offer a foundation to chart the company's likely future path, turning the exercise of prediction into a more informed and reliable tool for evaluating the business.

BUSINESS MODEL

In addition to the right size and fit, as well as a record of strong performance, the company's business model is another variable in evaluating the attractiveness of a target. Be on the lookout for certain features of a company's operations and revenue structure that confer a blend of stability, profitability, and reduced risk. Elements that are particularly attractive include

- flexible and scalable infrastructure with low marginal costs,
- ready access to a skilled workforce with minimal key person risk,
- recurring revenue among a diverse customer base,
- lean operation with agile outsourcing, and
- mitigated risks, including a broad supply network.

A flexible business model is one that is adaptable to market forces and one that grows without substantial investments in time and costs. Thus, scalability is different in brick-and-mortar businesses versus digital platforms or the hybrid model of bricks and clicks. Most of the time, the more a company relies on a physical presence and human employees, the longer it takes to grow, and this holds true whether you are selling services or products. Think about it—what can you replicate faster, a physical location or an online ordering and shipping platform?

A nimble and scalable business is one with a low **marginal cost**, which refers to its ability to produce an additional product or service without a significant increase in cost. This is most prevalent in digital companies but can also be found in manufacturing environments. Basically, a low marginal cost is possible whenever the cost of serving one additional customer is relatively negligible after the initial development and infrastructure investments have been made.

Your target's business model is also influenced by how skilled the workforce needs to be and how easy or difficult it would be to hire for key positions in the market(s) in which you want to operate. If a highly skilled professional is the linchpin to the business being successful—such as a subspecialty physician in a medical practice or a niche programmer in an IT business—the business's ability to duplicate its efforts through expansion will be limited and slow. Plus, if this key person leaves the company, the revenue will suffer until the employee is replaced. In SMB acquisitions facing a succession issue, this key person is often the founder or primary owner of the company. Founders can hold the metaphorical keys to the company's success, serving as the access point for its vision and strategy, institutional knowledge, and critical customer and supplier relationships. When this is the case, identify other executives with redundant skill sets and comparable business associations to reduce the risk associated with the founder's potential departure. Sellers with robust succession plans can ensure the company continues to thrive, even as leadership roles evolve.

Another important feature of an attractive target is its revenue model. Recurring revenue is a key indicator of financial health. It suggests that the company enjoys a steady and predictable stream of cash flow, providing a solid foundation for future growth and profitability. Look at the company's revenue stream(s), and check if the sales are a one-time occurrence or are/could be recurring, for example, through a subscription fee or proprietary replacement parts. A good example is the razor and blade business model, where the core product is sold at a deep discount, or even given away for free, in order to sell consumable supplies that can only be obtained from the same company. Anytime you can sell more products or services to the same customer base, your margin automatically goes up because you have little to no additional **customer acquisition cost (CAC)**. Customer loyalty and product differentiation matter here, too. If the company's customers love the product and do not want to get it anywhere else, or if the product is so unique that they *cannot* get it anywhere else, you have found a prime opportunity.

When evaluating the business model of an acquisition target, it's also crucial to consider the diversity of the company's customer base, as concentration in customer segments can significantly impact the target's risk profile and sustainability. Ideal acquisition targets are those whose earnings are generated from a broad customer base, minimizing the risk of significant revenue loss if one or more customers or customer types leave the business. As a rule of thumb, generating more than 20 percent of revenue from a single customer is considered risky; more than 30 percent is typically unacceptable. If you choose to move forward despite high customer concentration, you'll need to consider a deal structure that helps mitigate the risk of customer loss—more on that later.

A diverse customer base, coupled with multi-month or multi-year contracts, indicates a stable revenue stream. Even though a seller will likely not want to discuss names or specifics at this point, you should be able to get a high-level breakdown of the customer landscape. The goal of this process is to understand the company's unique value proposition—why customers choose it over competitors—and to evaluate how your value creation strategies, particularly pricing increases, might affect that dynamic. For example, would a price hike trigger a customer exodus, or is the company's offering strong enough to retain its client base? These questions are critical in assessing the reliability of the company's cash flow.

Another attractive element to seek in a target is how lean it runs its operation. Buyers with experience in manufacturing or other process-driven industries will recognize many familiar efficiency strategies. These principles apply broadly and have even gained traction in healthcare, particularly to improve patient throughput. In short, a lean operation strives to maximize customer value through attention to efficiency and waste reduction while using the least resources possible. Examples include eliminating redundant or unnecessary tasks, enhancing processes to avoid defects or rework, and amplifying productivity through disciplined use of resources.

One component of a lean company's resource efficiency is designing an asset-light business model—one that has a minimal amount of hard assets and capital investments in space and equipment but rather utilizes digital technologies and third-party outsourcing for noncore operations and physical plant needs. The premise here is that, by leveraging the assets and capabilities of external partners, the business can minimize fixed costs and maximize its flexibility to accommodate changing market conditions and support rapid scalability.

An asset-light business model relies on strategic partnerships and outsourcing to reduce capital expenditures and enhance the growth and agility of the business. This is particularly true when an activity is outside of the company's core competency. A perfect example is when universities and hospitals outsource their food service departments. Sure, they could outfit the kitchen and establish relationships with food and beverage suppliers, but this time and effort is likely better directed toward what they do best: educating students and providing patient care. Outsourcing avoids the cycle of hiring and training in-house staff to perform these specialized skills, thus promoting operational efficiency.

Interestingly, an asset-light business model has implications both before and after the acquisition. While we often say that people are a company's greatest asset—and they are, in terms of value—this refers specifically to physical or hard assets that could be sold on the open market, such as manufacturing equipment, vehicles, or real estate. These hard assets impact the investment prior to acquisition by influencing both the purchase price and the amount of capital you'll need to raise. Postacquisition, you'll need to service and eventually replace existing equipment—and often invest in new assets to support growth. There are pros and cons to owning versus outsourcing, but in many cases, leveraging an external partner is both faster and more cost-effective than purchasing and maintaining your own equipment, especially when factoring in depreciation and upkeep.

Finally, a strong business model is structured to mitigate other risks in addition to those already mentioned. Similar to the consequences of customer concentration, another significant risk is supplier concentration. A healthy business model features diversified sources of supply to mitigate the risks associated with supplier disruptions, price hikes, or quality issues. There has been no clearer illustration of this in recent memory than the supply chain issues related to the COVID-19 pandemic. To be sure, even the companies with the most diversified supplier networks still struggled during this global event, but the massive disruptions highlighted for everyone the need for redundant options in procuring key business product(s) and/or their component(s). Overreliance on a limited number of suppliers can jeopardize the company's ability to deliver products or services consistently and thus potentially impact cash flow and customer retention.

While not exhaustive, a sound operating model will address other business risks by encompassing

- diversified revenue streams to reduce dependency on a single product, service, or market;
- strategic B2B partnerships to provide access to new customers and product offerings;
- cybersecurity measures to protect against threats to an ever-increasing digital environment;
- regulatory compliance systems to monitor for changes and mitigate legal and reputational risks;
- customer-centric approaches to analyze and act upon customer feedback and market research; and
- a culture of innovation to support continuous improvement and novel business opportunities.

MARKET POSITIONING

Having the strongest business model possible is fantastic, but it doesn't mean a thing if the business has a declining market position. How your target company fits into the bigger picture of its industry is a critical component of its future success, as it impacts how the company is perceived in the market and its competitive standing. As a hockey fan (Go Preds!), I always refer to Wayne Gretzky's famous advice: "Skate where the puck is going, not where it has been." Your target could have had a Blockbuster past (pun intended), but will it be relevant and needed in ten years? If not, you might find yourself skating after a puck that's going nowhere. I've backed away from deals for exactly this reason.

Immediately before learning of the specialty pharmacy I ultimately acquired, I evaluated another specialty pharmacy treating a specific but widespread condition requiring lifelong medication. This target had all the right qualities—high customer loyalty with lots of recurring revenue and essentially no customer concentration. Likewise, it had margins north of 30 percent, primarily because they were able to operate with a lean staff in a very small footprint. The owner was another physician and was highly motivated to hand off the reins to a fellow doctor with a passion for serving the underserved. But there was one tiny problem ... Essentially all (at least 80 percent) of the revenue for these medications was coming through a lucrative government program that has been on the federal chopping block for almost a decade. If I had only looked at the business characteristics, I might have made a poor decision—but because my industry knowledge allowed for an understanding of the policy landscape, I was able to kindly pass on that opportunity.

The "hockey puck assessment" should compel you to be disciplined against seeking out the hot thing and encourage you to instead study industry headwinds and tailwinds so that you choose wisely, rather than chasing something that is flashy or in vogue. Spoiler alert: Good acquisition targets are frequently boring or super niche businesses that you have never heard of. When acquiring a business, dull is good, even when it comes to financial performance—proof of growth is necessary, but that does not have to entail spectacular year-over-year increases. You are looking for a consistent base of repeat customers, with room to expand through new customers, markets, and enhanced product offerings for years to come.

In addition to a few industry-specific characteristics, all businesses can be evaluated using several common features of a strong market position, which can indicate how your target company stands out in the competitive landscape. These include

- recognizing competitors,

- comparing pricing,
- understanding switching costs,
- examining loyalty,
- assessing reputation,
- determining distribution channels, and
- identifying alliances.

Understanding who your target's competitors are is a fundamental step. This involves identifying direct and indirect competitors in the market and analyzing their strengths and weaknesses. The **confidential information memorandum (CIM)** that you receive on the acquisition opportunity will almost certainly address competition, and you should add to this by doing a little research of your own. In addition to online queries, call your industry-specific contacts throughout the country and ask who they are seeing and hearing about in this space, and be sure to consider disruptive competitors, such as artificial intelligence (AI), automation, and offshoring.

Alongside this, a pricing comparison is crucial. How your target company prices its products or services in relation to its competitors can significantly influence its appeal to customers. Remember, it is not just about being cheaper but rather about offering value that resonates with the target market. Take into consideration any historical pricing changes the company has made and try to assess how, or if, these shifts in pricing affected the company's position among its competitors.

Another pivotal aspect in determining a target's position in the market is to assess both barriers to entry and switching costs. These factors determine how easy or difficult it is for new competitors to enter the market and for customers to switch to a competitor. High barriers to entry, such as substantial initial investments in machinery or technology or onerous regulatory or licensing requirements, can protect a company's market position, creating a proverbial moat around the castle of the business.

Similarly, significant switching costs—how difficult or expensive it is for customers to use a different company's product—can discourage them from moving to a competitor, thereby enhancing the loyalty of your consumer base. This is most heavily driven by the factor that compels customers to choose your target company over another: its unique value proposition. This defining feature could be an innovative aspect, over-the-top customer service, or a socially driven cause. It is what resonates with the company's fans.

In addition, factors such as brand reputation and product quality are, of course, critical to a company's market position, as are the channels through which it distributes its products or services. Physical channels, such as retail stores, and digital channels, such as e-commerce platforms, are important to define. The more extensive and efficient the distribution channels, the better the access to customers.

Finally, the partners and allies with whom the target company collaborates play a crucial role in strengthening its position. These relationships not only expand market reach but also leverage each partner's expertise to enhance product offerings and drive innovation. Such strategic alliances open doors to untapped markets and new customer segments, solidifying the company's competitive edge.

VALUE CREATION

Finally, a core component of deciding if your target company is the right fit for you is assessing the potential opportunities for you to add value to the business, thus increasing your returns in both the short term, during the holding period, and the long term, at the eventual exit. I think of value creation in a business much like renovating a house: It both enhances your experience of living there and then generates an outsized return when you sell it.

When it comes to flipping a house, you can attract more potential buyers and garner a higher sales price by expanding the square footage, repairing or improving unsightly parts, and adding upgraded features. These value-adding actions are similar to the four primary ways to add value to a company:

1. Get more customers.
2. Generate more revenue.
3. Improve the product.
4. Optimize your process.

Everyone knows that the most elemental approach for growing a business is to sell more, right?! Indeed, getting more customers and selling more products to those customers are two key approaches to value creation in your target company. First, expanding your customer base is a crucial aspect of growing an acquired business, which can be achieved through several strategies. This could mean geographic expansion through adding sales reps or additional locations in new markets, and it also could take the form of expanding your reach to new demographic segments in the same geography by adapting your offerings to suit cultural or age-related preferences. By identifying new markets and untapped customer segments, you can introduce your products or services to a broader audience. Additionally, partnerships and collaborations can open up new markets and customer bases. By partnering with complementary businesses or industry influencers, you can tap into their audiences and gain credibility through association.

Secondly, leveraging various marketing channels, particularly online platforms, can significantly boost your reach. Utilizing social media, search engine optimization, and email marketing allows you to connect with customers where they spend a lot of their time. While this might seem like a terribly obvious approach, you should not assume that small business owners are leveraging these low-cost, effective options, as many longtime owners/operators are still relying on the same marketing channels (newspaper, fax) that worked for them ten to fifteen years ago. In fact, you should apply the "fax machine test" to identify businesses that can quickly create value simply by modernizing their communication and outreach strategies.

Once you have customers, whether old or new, you have to keep them coming back for more! Improving retention of customers is just as important as recruiting new ones, and exceptional customer service is key to keeping the company's current customers happy and loyal. Dig deep into how your target responds to customer inquiries or complaints to assess customer satisfaction and identify opportunities to reduce attrition. Moreover, in many industries, you can add loyalty programs, including early access and exclusive discounts, that reward repeat customers and encourage them to keep coming back. By combining these strategies, you can not only attract more customers but also ensure they remain engaged and loyal over time, significantly boosting the business's growth and profitability.

Basic business principles also dictate that selling more products, or generating more revenue from the same products, is the quickest way to enhance profitability because of little or no incremental customer acquisition cost. This revenue boost from an existing customer base can be strategically achieved through both pricing increases and cross-selling opportunities. A carefully considered pricing increase is a tactic that almost instantly and wholly accrues to the bottom line. Small business owners, particularly founders, may not have changed pricing in years, despite their own expenses increasing over the same time period. This resistance is generally driven by a fear of losing customers, but regular reassessment of one's pricing strategy is a good practice in all industries. During your diligence, arm yourself with data in your determination of what the market can support. Consider how much **pricing power** (the ability to increase prices with marginal or no loss of customers) your target company may have by using industry benchmarks, as well as the company's experience with previous price increases.

Likewise, a company can enhance its revenue by cross-selling additional products or upselling premium services to existing customers. By offering complementary products to your target customers, you can enhance their experience while increasing your average sales price per customer. For instance, if a customer buys a laptop, offering them a compatible carrying case or software can be a smart cross-sell. Upselling is another potent strategy that encourages customers to purchase upgraded services or premium features. This could involve offering add-ons that enhance the core product's functionality or suggesting a more comprehensive service package. It is essential to show the added value these premium options provide to persuade customers effectively. By bundling products or services together at a discounted rate, customers perceive that they are getting better value for their money, which can encourage them to purchase more than they initially intended.

Another value creation strategy lies in improving the product or service that the company already sells. Although you may not perceive your target company's product as "broken" (and therefore not in need of "fixing"), one of the most effective ways to create value is by enhancing the product. This can be achieved with quality and design improvements or by adding innovative features. It's very likely that employees and customers can instantly tell you the product's pain points and competitive disadvantages. With such stakeholder feedback and a look at market trends, you can thoughtfully refine the product's design, increasing its functionality and attractiveness. This not only makes the product more appealing to your customers but also ensures your product remains relevant and desirable in the competitive market.

A final key strategy for adding value to an acquired business is optimizing its efficiency. SMBs can be notoriously inefficient, especially if they are still led by the founder. You may quickly identify ways to improve efficiency in staffing patterns, such as in a scenario where specialized, skilled workers are performing general or administrative tasks. This bad habit starts innocently with a "get it done" attitude by hardworking, roll-up-your-sleeves employees. However, it often morphs into highly compensated professionals performing duties, such as ordering supplies or making routine callbacks, that could easily be handled by a lower-paid administrative staffer. To maximize operational efficiency, make sure that each employee is focused on only the things they are uniquely qualified to handle. In healthcare, we call this "working at the top of one's license."

Along these same lines, founder-led businesses may still be relying upon processes that have not been updated in years. This is often driven by the "if it's not broken" mentality and exacerbated by the investment required to upgrade technology or automate tasks. Whereas not every manual process should be discarded, most businesses can gain efficiencies through the integration of software and automation. This not only speeds up processes but also reduces waste and errors, thus allowing staff to focus on more strategic tasks that add greater value. Finally, by analyzing and refining every step of the supply chain, from sourcing raw materials to delivering the final product to the customers, you can identify opportunities for cost savings and quicker delivery times.

Red Flags and Dealbreakers to Keep in Mind as You Move Ahead

Now that you have defined the criteria for your acquisition, your goal should be to apply these standards to each target and rule out unqualified companies as quickly as possible. Again, the goal here is to fail fast so you do not waste time or resources on a bad deal. Even if they make the initial cut, potential target companies should be scanned for red flags and early warning signs that indicate the business has risks that may be dealbreakers, even at a great acquisition price.

Red flags that could indicate underlying problems or risks with the investment include

- inconsistencies in financial records;
- elusive or contradictory communication;
- significant customer concentration;
- legal, environmental, or regulatory issues;
- obsolete processes or technology;
- high employee turnover rates; and/or
- overreliance on the owner's participation.

Recognizing these red flags early in the acquisition process allows buyers to make more informed decisions, negotiate better terms, or decide to walk away from a deal that poses too many risks—something I've done myself.

A searcher once approached me about investing in a private-duty nursing business in a high-net-worth (HNW) coastal city. The nurse–owner wanted to retire and sell the business. The company had built a discreet, concierge-style model over two decades, serving a small but loyal group of celebrity and affluent clients, and had grown to over $1.5 million in EBITDA. With no marketing or public footprint, the business relied entirely on word-of-mouth referrals from a few trusted physicians. The owner claimed that she "didn't really do anything" beyond taking calls from doctors and matching clients with nurses, suggesting the business could be easily transferred, even to a non-clinician. On the surface, it seemed like a straightforward, high-margin opportunity.

However, at least three key risks made it a dealbreaker for me. First, compliance risk—were these nurses operating within their scope of practice and within state law, or was there potential regulatory exposure? Second, customer concentration risk—with a client base primarily consisting of elderly, long-term patients, could the business replace them as quickly as attrition naturally occurred? Third, key person risk—the company's success was built entirely on the owner's personal relationships, none of which would automatically transfer to a new buyer.

While the financials looked strong and the business model was low-cost and simple, the underlying risks were significant. When looking to acquire a business, evaluating these structural vulnerabilities is just as important as assessing profitability. With these red flags and dealbreakers in mind, you can move on to the exciting next step: finding your new business. The next chapter explains how it's done.

CHAPTER 4

HOW TO FIND YOUR NEW BUSINESS

"I am a great believer in luck. The harder I work, the more of it I seem to have."[12]

—Coleman Cox

You should now be pretty clear on why you want to pursue SMB ownership and have an idea of the kind of businesses that would make for a suitable target. But where do you find companies for sale? Unlike real estate, there generally are no descriptive website listings, advertisements, and yard signs for businesses, and, by and large, businesses promoted in this manner are usually less desirable. Attractive targets are typically held close to the vest and must be sought out, sometimes in a secretive and competitive manner.

Like most things in life, you've got to do your homework if you want to find something great. There will be lots of businesses that look great on the surface, but when you dig deeper, you'll realize they are

12 Cox, Coleman. *Listen to This.* San Francisco: Coleman Cox Publishing Co., 1922, 15.

not the right fit for you. Much like the process of finding the love of your life, you'll have to go on several dates (and maybe even kiss a few frogs!) before you find "the one." Similarly, when finding a business to acquire, you've got to dedicate yourself to the search. Most successful acquirers evaluate upwards of one hundred companies, talk to twenty to thirty sellers, and present three to five LOIs before closing a deal.

As we dive into where to source these businesses, it is useful to define what kind of buyer you are. This will help frame your search and direct you to the most fruitful sources. Speaking of search—not everyone who is looking to buy a business uses a traditional search fund vehicle, but all acquisition entrepreneurs could generally be referred to as searchers, because in many respects, the process follows the same cadence: First, you need to fund the search, and then, you need to raise acquisition capital.

Search Funds and Entrepreneurship Through Acquisition

A search fund is a relatively new investment vehicle that allows investors to finance an entrepreneur's efforts to identify, acquire, and operate a privately held company. The concept was born in the 1980s at Ivy League business schools—most notably Stanford, but also Yale and Harvard—and is becoming a wildly popular asset class because of its high returns and mitigated risks compared to start-ups. Search funds are also a fast track to entrepreneurship for individuals with strong managerial skills and have become the cornerstone of ETA programs; thus, the terms are often used interchangeably.

Whether formal or informal, the process of acquiring a business typically unfolds in two distinct phases. The first phase in a **traditional search fund** involves search capital, where funds are raised from investors to cover the costs associated with a searcher taking on a full-time role in finding and evaluating potential acquisition targets, usually for up to two years. This includes salary, travel, due diligence, and other related expenses. But not everyone will want to pursue the traditional search fund model—you could be searching full-time and paying search expenses through savings or even looking for an acquisition target while you are working a full-time job. If so, you would be leading a **self-funded search**.

Once a suitable business is identified, your search enters its second phase, which involves raising acquisition capital. Whether or not you had external financing for your search phase, this larger, second tranche of funds is used to finance the actual purchase of the company. In a traditional search fund model, investors who help fund the initial search capital are financially incentivized to "follow on" in the acquisition round. To reward them for their early risk and support, their initial investment typically receives a **step-up** in value—usually by 1.5×—when it's rolled into the acquisition, meaning it's treated as if it were 1.5 times its original value when applied toward the purchase.

Remember, the acquisition capital used to purchase your target is typically broken down into two sources: **debt**, the amount you borrow from a lender or possibly the seller, and **equity**, the investment of cash brought to the deal. Chapters 7 and 8 elaborate on debt and equity financing and their sources. For now, it's important to figure out what type of buyer you are.

Types of Buyers

Knowing how to position yourself as a buyer will prepare you to answer one of the initial questions you are likely to get as a first-time acquirer: Where are you getting the funds for this acquisition? While this may seem like a rude question, the seller (or, more likely, their representative) is attempting to do the exact same thing you are—weed out unqualified leads as quickly as possible. To define your acquisition approach and signify your ability to afford the transaction, determine which of the following buyer categories fits you best.

SELF-FUNDED SEARCHERS

Self-funded searchers are individuals or small teams looking to acquire businesses, typically with less than $2 million in EBITDA. Unlike the traditional searcher described below, these buyers enter the acquisition process without initial external investment in the search phase, choosing instead to fund their own search, covering personal expenses and initial acquisition costs through their regular job income and/or personal savings. After target identification, equity for acquisition is usually funded through personal savings, as well as external capital raised from friends and family, HNW individuals who are accredited investors, and possibly small institutional investors. Debt financing most often comes from SBA loans, traditional bank financing, or seller notes. Ultimately, the self-funded approach allows the buyer to retain full control and flexibility during the search and acquisition process, stay closely involved in evaluating and selecting the right business, and delay or avoid the need to bring in outside investors until a deal is secured.

TRADITIONAL SEARCH FUNDS

Traditional search funds operate on a slightly larger scale, targeting businesses with $1 million–$5 million in EBITDA. These funds raise initial capital, commonly ranging from $400,000 to $800,000, to support the search process itself, while the searcher works full-time to find an attractive target. Search capital is raised according to an aligned investment thesis, ensuring the investors and searcher agree on ideal target qualities and a defined time frame (usually twenty-four months). Once a target is identified, the fund raises additional equity from the initial investors—who often receive that step-up incentive mentioned previously—and potentially other investors as well. Debt financing is typically sourced from traditional institutional lenders, while equity funding comes from HNW individuals and institutional investors. This model allows for a structured search process with the financial backing to pursue a wider range of acquisition opportunities.

Historically, traditional search funds have been launched by recent MBA graduates, often encouraged by student groups and experienced professors at their institutions. Over the last few years, there has been a noticeable shift toward mid-career professionals launching search funds, bringing with them a wealth of hands-on experience and perhaps a more nuanced understanding of business operations. I witnessed the shift firsthand when I attended a Harvard ETA conference, where I was old enough to be the average attendee's mother. Many there assumed I was an investor, only to show surprise and confusion when they learned I was, like them, a searcher. This experience highlighted the persisting stereotype of younger, newly minted MBA grads dominating the field, even as the landscape begins to evolve.

INDEPENDENT SPONSORS

Independent sponsors represent a more flexible and scalable approach to acquisitions, targeting businesses of any size but usually concentrating on those with more than $2 million EBITDA. Unlike self-funded searchers or traditional search funds, independent sponsors operate with a more formalized process, securing institutional debt and equity financing on a deal-specific basis. Because the independent sponsor model can involve complex structuring and intricate financing arrangements, this approach is often too daunting for a first-time buyer.

This acquisition model is akin to traditional private equity (PE), with the primary difference being sponsors raising funds on a deal-by-deal basis versus tapping into a ready pool of capital awaiting deployment from the PE fund. Thus, independent sponsors are often referred to as "fundless sponsors," a term I have always disliked because it sounds like "FUN-less," which is certainly not the case! For experienced buyers, the independent sponsor model offers a high degree of flexibility for both the buyer and the seller, allowing for creativity and customization of individual deal terms.

FINANCIAL BUYERS AND STRATEGIC BUYERS

To round out the description of buyer types, there are two other prominent players in the SMB acquisition space: **financial buyers**, including PE funds and family offices, and **strategic buyers**.

Financial buyers are institutions that are in the business of buying companies. Such buyers bring a predefined investment perspective, set of objectives, and strategy to the acquisition process, which are collectively referred to as the fund's **investment mandate**. **PE funds** raise a pool of capital from limited partners to invest in businesses that meet certain numeric and mission-driven criteria. Limited partners commit capital to a dedicated fund managed by professional investors (the **general partner**) who seek to acquire companies aligned with a specific investment thesis. When these investors manage wealth on behalf of the heirs of an ultrawealthy family or group of families, the firm is known as a **family office**, which often deploys capital thematically. These funds have the resources, often in the tens to hundreds of millions of dollars, to acquire and manage multiple businesses and frequently look for companies with strong growth potential or turnaround opportunities.

Strategic buyers, on the other hand, are existing companies seeking to acquire synergistic businesses to integrate into their existing operations. Often known as platform companies, these buyers aim to expand their market presence, create efficiencies, add a new product or service, and/or enter new markets through acquisitions. The smaller businesses that get folded into the platform are commonly called **roll-ups** or **tuck-ins**.

Search Strategy

When searching for an SMB to acquire, there are two primary search strategies: brokered searches and proprietary searches. Each has its own distinct advantages and challenges. Both methods have respectable standings in the landscape of SMB acquisition, and there is no right or wrong method to choose. Combining the two approaches often yields the widest variety of potential targets, so do not get stuck going down only one avenue. Your search strategy ultimately depends on your resources, expertise, network, and strategic preferences.

BROKERED SEARCHES

Brokered searches use the power of intermediaries such as business brokers, mergers and acquisitions (M&A) advisors, or investment bankers to identify investment opportunities. Just like in real estate, there are buy-side and sell-side advisors who serve as agents to the people who retain them. These professionals earn a commission or success fee when an acquisition is successfully transacted—similar to how agents are compensated in other deal-driven industries. And, as with real estate, the quality of the broker or advisor can vary widely, literally making or breaking the deal, so do your homework when choosing one!

If you can get multiple people on the lookout for your search target, your reach expands exponentially—that's exactly what building relationships with brokers will do. They're not hard to find at industry socials, such as events hosted by the Association for Corporate Growth (ACG), M&A conferences, and capital connection events. However, in my experience, many brokers are selective about who they share their listings with, and some may even have reservations about search funds because of past negative experiences. That's why investing time in building genuine relationships with brokers and M&A advisors is critical. Learn about their background (pro tip: this is usually not their first career), understand the types of deals they prefer (size, industry, structure), and get to know them on a personal level.

Intermediary compensation can vary, but fee structures typically include a lump sum success fee or a percentage-based commission at closing, sometimes paired with an initial retainer. Despite the additional cost it incurs, the brokered search method offers several benefits over proprietary searches: steady deal flow, higher-quality deals, and credibility and expertise in negotiations.

In order to effectively engage with brokers, you must demonstrate that you are a serious and financially ready buyer, usually by sharing your investment thesis and loan prequalification letter if you are a first-time acquirer. The level of scrutiny and access to information vary with the size of the deal and the type of broker. Business brokers generally focus on small business transactions under $5 million enterprise value; they will often publish a listing of businesses available for sale, sometimes with the asking price listed. M&A advisors and investment bankers typically represent larger deals, primarily in the lower middle market—those with an enterprise value of at least $10 million—and are usually quite selective when sharing information about the clients they represent. In short, the bigger the deal, the higher the bar for being considered a competitive prospective buyer.

Once you close a deal through a broker—trust me, they'll remember you—you better believe you'll be the first call when a potential tuck-in opportunity pops up (a **tuck-in acquisition** is when a larger company fully absorbs a smaller one, which can be a powerful way to scale your business inorganically). Building strong broker relationships puts you at the front of the line for getting early looks at such prime deals.

Call me old-fashioned, but these relationships are best built in person. Even if your initial introduction is virtual, take the extra step to meet in person when you're nearby. I've dropped off cookies at a banker's office while in Dallas for a conference, met an advisor and his junior associate for coffee during a work trip in Atlanta, and even arranged a rooftop happy hour with a broker when vacationing in Palm Springs. These small gestures go a long way—because they build the kind of relationships where you can pick up the phone and get real-time insights into what intermediaries are seeing in the market, both in their own deals and across their networks.

PROPRIETARY SEARCHES

Proprietary searches involve directly reaching out to business owners without the assistance of intermediaries, such as investment bankers or business brokers. In this approach, using publicly available data supplemented with personal knowledge and perhaps paid database access, the searcher creates lists of business owners within specific industries and/or geographies at which to direct their cold outreach. With the aid of AI, offshoring, and other technology tools now available, searchers can send literally hundreds of emails per day in a shotgun-style approach. While this tactic is low-cost and wide-reaching, its response rate is depressingly low, generally in the 1 to 2 percent range. Given that SMB owners across several industries have reported receiving an average of one email per week soliciting the sale of their business, it is admittedly difficult to get your email to stand out amongst the crowd. Likewise, it is a stretch for many business owners to begin discussing the divestiture of their life's work with a stranger on the internet.

Even when you do get a bite using this approach, the quality of the target may not be all that desirable. Instead of randomly discovering the rare business owner at just the right time who has been mentally and organizationally preparing to sell their company, you are more likely to encounter someone in the very early stages of shopping around and testing the waters of valuation. Undoubtedly, such a business owner has read news articles or heard stories from country club buddies of how they sold their companies for tens of millions of dollars and is using your outreach as an opportunity to see what they could get in an exit. These potential targets often do not have their financials ready to share and will require weeks to compile sufficient data for you to properly value the company. Even if the conversation does reach this point, one or both of you may discover that there is not a good fit between your respective sets of ideals, values, and personalities—all key components to concluding a successful transaction and transition.

Still, do not be discouraged from pursuing proprietary outreach! Sourcing a deal on your own can help you avoid the fees and bidding wars (both associated with a higher ultimate purchase price) inherent to brokered deals. In addition to online prospecting, use existing and local resources to source an acquisition target directly. As you know, in any kind of new business relationship, a warm intro from a mutual colleague goes much further than cold outreach ever will, and the same applies here. When you are on the hunt for a business to acquire, I recommend you tell *everyone*—industry contacts, professional networks, trade association representatives, accountants, local chambers of commerce, legal and financial advisors, friends, neighbors, and fellow parishioners. I promise that asking them to help you identify a business to acquire will be such an unusual and impressive request that they will keep an ear to the ground for you and pass along anything that sounds consistent with your intended target. You may even consider enticing them with a finder's fee if they source a company that you end up acquiring.

ONLINE RESOURCES

In every industry, you can garner a good start to both proprietary offerings and brokered deals by exploring online sources. While online listings generally tend to be lower-quality deals, they're still a great way to gauge the market, understand valuation trends, and, occasionally, uncover a diamond in the rough worth pursuing. The suggestions below are examples of various repositories to consider—this is not an all-inclusive or endorsed list but represents the primary players at the time of writing. Specifically, for SMBs available for acquisition, here are some key online platforms to check:

Business marketplaces: BizBuySell, BusinessesForSale, BizQuest, LoopNet, BusinessBroker, Empire Flippers, SideProjectors, IndieMaker, Acquire, LINK Business, First Choice Business Brokers, Motion Invest, Latona's, Investors Club, Synergy Business Brokers

M&A online platforms: DealStream, Flippa, Website Closers, Quiet Light, SMERGERS, Benchmark International, FE International, X5 Deals

Deal aggregators: Axial, Interexo, BizNexus, The SMB List, Centurica's Marketwatch, PrivSource, Rejigg, Grata

Online SMB acquisition communities: SEARCHFUNDER, The Business Inquirer, Kumo, SMBacquire

Many of the sites listed above offer free email distribution list subscriptions, newsletters, and online forums. You may want to sign up for several of these and spend the early weeks of your search perusing listings and reading discussion boards to learn the lingo and rhythm of searching and acquiring. As you get a clearer picture of your specific industry and/or geography of focus, consider setting up alerts on these platforms to notify you of new listings matching your requirements so you can act quickly on potential opportunities.

You've Found "The One"—What's Next?

While I discuss financing best practices in later chapters, I want to emphasize that fundraising is a process that starts sooner rather than later—as in, now! You will need to have a financing plan in place by the time you issue your LOI at the very latest, but ideally sooner. I suggest figuring out your funding sources as soon as you have identified a serious acquisition target and have conducted preliminary due diligence. I discuss financing types in chapter 7 and best practices for equity fundraising in chapter 8.

Now that you have found an attractive target, you will need a general understanding of the overall deal process to keep the components and timelines of each step in perspective. Speaking of timing, one thing you should know up front: This process will take much longer than you want or expect—it is measured in weeks and months, not days. The marathon versus sprint analogy is accurate here, and your pacing and expectations should be consistent with a daily slog that feels never-ending. Fortunately, it *does* eventually end, and you will soon forget the pain of the transaction once the joy of new business ownership takes over. The next chapter takes you through the stages of acquiring your target company.

RN BOR

TURAL-

BORN

RAL-N

CHAPTER 5

THE STAGES OF A DEAL

"Nothing great is achieved without much enduring."[13]

—*St. Catherine of Siena*

You have spent dozens of hours reaching out to business owners and combing through online listings, done your market research on the industry and geography, and *finally* found something that looks compelling enough to take the next step ... So now what? The fundamental steps in going from expressing interest in buying a business to locking down exclusivity as a buyer generally follow the same course: expressing initial interest, completing preliminary due diligence, gaining a deeper understanding of the business, and making a formal offer.

As a whole, the process could be viewed as the business equivalent of going from seeing an attractive online dating profile to getting engaged. It is a loosely choreographed dance that, without a smooth and orderly progression through the generally accepted phases, could lead to a breakup—or, worse, leave you on one knee, ring in hand,

13 "7 Quotes from St. Catherine of Siena," Ascension Press, April 26, 2019, https://media.ascensionpress.com/2019/04/26/7-quotes-from-st-catherine-of-siena/.

with your would-be sweetheart shaking their head. To avoid such a scenario, let's go through the typical stages of a deal.

Process for Expressing Interest

Expressing initial interest involves introducing yourself as a potential buyer and requesting more detailed information about the target company. If you sourced the business through an online marketplace or brokerage, you probably do not know the name of the company or its exact location, as you'll likely have only seen a "blind listing" with a vaguely descriptive pseudonym (say, "Project Aqua" for a pool company) and broad geography (region or state). Before you can access any identifiable information about the target, you must sign a **nondisclosure agreement (NDA)**, which protects the confidentiality of the sensitive data you are about to receive. While most NDAs are boilerplate, you may want an attorney to review the document before signing, especially if it includes terms that could limit your future work in the field (unlikely, but possible). Hold on to each NDA you sign, as you will need to reference it if you later send an LOI.

Once the NDA is signed, you will receive a **confidential information memorandum** (**CIM**, pronounced "sim"), an in-depth document containing detailed information about the company. Common components include

- an overview and history of the business,
- background on the owner with rationale for selling,
- a detailed description of the company's products and services,
- highlights of its unique value proposition,
- specifics on the industry and competitive environment,
- an overview of key operational and financial data, and
- the structure of management and employees.

Some CIM slide decks may also include strategic growth opportunities, anticipated risks going forward, and preferences regarding the terms of the deal. Often crafted by an intermediary, such as a broker or M&A advisor, the quality and granularity of CIMs vary according to the sophistication and resources of the author. In any case, a CIM is a crucial piece of the early diligence process, allowing you to make an informed decision on whether or not to pursue a transaction. There is no harm in reviewing lots of CIMs—in fact, you should, especially in the early days of your search. Assessing CIMs from multiple businesses will enhance your familiarity with what information should be in there, so you can easily identify missing details in future reviews. Likewise, if you're focused on a particular industry, reviewing multiple CIMs will give you valuable insight into the competitive landscape, common business models, and key differentiators across companies.

If you are encouraged by what you learn in a CIM and want to continue the pursuit, the next step usually involves a conversation with the intermediary, unless the seller is representing the deal directly. In this first interaction with the broker or advisor, you will learn more about the business and the seller—and at the same time, your suitability as a potential buyer will be evaluated. The first impression can make or break the deal, so come prepared to sell yourself: Present a professional background, describe your ability to acquire the company, and ask insightful preliminary diligence questions.

After this initial conversation, you'll likely have additional, more nuanced questions—especially related to financial details and operational metrics—as you evaluate the strategic fit of the target company. The next step is often for the intermediary to arrange a virtual meeting with the seller to address those questions and begin building rapport. However, if there is a wide pool of interest, the broker may suggest you participate in an **indication of interest (IOI)** process before directly interacting with the seller. An IOI is used by potential buyers to formally express interest in possibly acquiring the target company after they have reviewed the CIM. An IOI serves as a nonbinding expression of your interest in pursuing the transaction and offers a high-level view of your proposed deal structure and valuation range. The seller, usually represented by an intermediary, will dictate whether an IOI is required or not—if one is asked for, you should submit it. This basically helps to weed out the tire kickers and is used in competitive processes when multiple parties are interested. It can also help gauge market pricing and position the seller to secure the best overall deal—balancing price, terms, and strategic fit.

It's worth dedicating time to the IOI, as it will also serve as the basis for a subsequent LOI. A typical IOI is no more than one to two pages and covers the following points:

- **Introduction:** Start with an introduction to yourself and your background, specifically as it pertains to the target company's industry. Note any experience you have with previous business acquisitions.
- **Expression of interest:** Clearly indicate your interest in acquiring the specific company and consider adding a line or two about why the opportunity is intriguing to you.
- **Plan for valuing and financing the deal:** Describe an approximate price range that you believe you could support, and articulate the source of funds that can back up your preliminary offer.
- **Transition plan:** Finish the letter with a high-level overview of the seller's transition and your postclosing plan.
- **Next steps:** Sign the letter with a call to action to move to the next step.

- **Follow up:** When putting together your IOI, give the seller or broker a call and let them know it's coming. Reiterate your interest, and ask when you might hear back—it could be minutes or weeks.

As you are contemplating the terms and pricing you want to include in your IOI, a wise move would be to have a conversation with the broker or advisor about what the seller expects and/or any non-negotiables in the transaction. You may or may not be able to solicit details on pricing, as some sellers want to keep numbers discussions open-ended in order to get the highest bids possible. Even if you don't get hard figures, you will likely hear about other pertinent priorities of the seller. These could be simple things that do not matter much to you or that you were already planning, such as deal structure, timing, or employee retention. You may also uncover key deal terms that could significantly impact the price—such as whether the seller requires the real estate to be part of the sale or if you have the option to lease it postclosing. This line of questioning may reveal unreasonable demands that would be a nonstarter for you. It is better to know this now, so you can tap out before expending additional time and resources.

Moving to the Next Round

When submitting your IOI, your goal is to be deemed part of the pool of sufficiently competitive and capable potential buyers. This group, which often represents up to half of the initial respondents, is then invited to participate in the next round. In this phase, you may get access to the **virtual data room (VDR**, or just **data room** for short), where the seller will upload financial, legal, and operational documents for your review. The primary aim is to verify what you assumed in the initial review, as well as to look for red flags. If you identify a dealbreaker at any time in the diligence process, walk away. Do not let the emotional excitement of a potential purchase cloud your judgment.

Whether it is in preliminary (early) or confirmatory (later) due diligence, I like the order of documents to follow the **FLO—Financial, Legal, and Operational**. If the financial documents do not check out, why should you care about the legal contracts? And if you are hitting legal or regulatory roadblocks, why bother drilling down into employee benefits and sales bonuses?

At this point, you will likely have the opportunity to meet with the seller—initially virtually, but eventually in person, typically on-site at the business. I strongly recommend visiting the site as early in the process as possible. If a visit isn't offered, you should request one. It is amazing how much better you can wrap your head around the business by seeing and experiencing in real life what you have read on paper. This meeting could be held alone with the seller or include select members of the management team who are aware of the potential sale. Depending on the level of management team knowledge regarding the transaction, as well as the curiosity of employees who see you there, the seller may introduce you as anything from the potential buyer of the company to a "consultant" or "visiting colleague."

Beyond a site visit, it's also good practice to expand your meeting to a more informal environment, such as a lunch or dinner. This opens the opportunity to casually include partners or spouses. I think you can glean a lot of intangible data from getting to know someone's spouse or partner. When I've used this tactic, I have invariably picked up social cues that reveal personality traits and value systems that directly impact the business. For example, one of my sellers talked over their partner and restated any negative information in a more positive light. That translated into a culture where employees didn't feel empowered to speak up about bad news and instead sugarcoated everything for the boss, even if it wasn't necessarily rooted in reality.

Regardless of the setting and attendees, some critical components should be covered in this first conversation. You know what they say about first impressions, so this is your chance to nail it. To do so, come prepared with a solid background knowledge of the business, based not only on the documents you have been poring over but also your industry and market research. Do your homework and be ready with thoughtful questions and discussion topics. But remember, this is not an interrogation—and you are *not* there to flex your position as a potential buyer and your ability to deploy capital! Instead of firing questions one after another, keep the conversation flowing by asking open-ended questions, delving deeper into any recurring themes, and listening for points that are implied or left unsaid. Here is an overview of key items you'll want to get the seller's perspective on:

- **Business overview:** Ask the seller about the business history, mission, and core values, as well as any sentinel events. You might also ask about the seller's/company's involvement in the community, for example, through charitable organizations.
- **Products/services and customers:** Get more details about the company's products and services, as well as the characteristics of its customer base, especially any potential customer instability and/or concentration.
- **Financial performance trends:** This information should include any current financial issues or obligations, plus high-level projections on upcoming headwinds and tailwinds.
- **Industry dynamics and market forecast:** Touch on key competitors and the business's unique value proposition. This conversation should also touch on legal and regulatory issues, past, present, and future.

- **Key operational components:** This includes technology, infrastructure, and employees. When it comes to employees, another thing that you need to figure out is the undercurrent of relationships within the business. I'm not talking about general office politics but actual family or romantic relationships among employees, specifically those in leadership positions.
- **Seller's deal expectations:** Discuss the seller's expectations for the valuation and timing of the sale, as well as the postclosing transition and their possible ongoing involvement in the company.
- **Potential reputational concerns:** You will have to tread lightly here, as you want to avoid embarrassing the seller by being too direct or intrusive. You might ask about media coverage they have received or inquire vaguely about any "distractions" from the business they can recall through the years.

Remember, this conversation is just as much a matter of the seller evaluating you as it is you vetting the seller and their business. I like to think of this first interaction as an interview for a CEO role, so be prepared to showcase your competence and experience while demonstrating what a good partner you will be. Prepare to cover

- your background,
- why this particular business interests you,
- the deal structure you envision,
- who your investors are, and
- how quickly you intend to close the deal.

Something to keep on your radar during this meeting is to ascertain just how involved the seller is in the business. Many sellers underplay the level of their day-to-day work in the business in a good-hearted attempt to reassure the buyer that their learning curve and time commitment will be manageable after acquisition. This is hardly ever done in the vein of deceit—rather, the seller has been doing it for so long and is so ingrained in daily operations that they do not realize how critical they are to the company's daily functioning. One way to identify this is to watch how the seller interacts in a management team meeting; if their executives rely on them for answers on multiple fronts, then their absence from the company may be acutely felt after the sale.

Finally, remember that this first in-person meeting is just as much about building trust as it is getting information, so approach it with a professional and respectful attitude. Remember, you are asking to carry on the owner's legacy. Because of the sentimental ties the seller almost certainly has to the company and its employees, this interaction may be emotional for them, so grace and understanding are appreciated.

After the first on-site visit, it is normal to feel overwhelmed and exhausted! Once you clear your head, look back at the (hopefully copious) notes you took during the conversations and confirm any assumptions you made from the documents. If new data points or concerns surfaced during the discussion, promptly request any clarifying information you need to complete your analysis.

Writing a Letter of Intent

With a better understanding of the business, rapport with the seller, and a good idea of how you will operate and grow the company, you are ready to compose a **letter of intent (LOI)** with your offer to purchase the business. Although the LOI is technically nonbinding, there are portions of the document that can have future implications if not carefully written, so you should solicit professional advice before proceeding. If you plan to use an SBA lender, the loan broker can help with the first draft of your LOI. However, to help you craft the finished product, you will have to incur some expense—by which I mean, hire a good lawyer who specializes in M&A (not the guy who negotiated your divorce or your last home purchase). An attorney with M&A experience can help you see around corners that would not otherwise be on your radar, and, although often costly, a good transaction attorney is worth their weight in gold. I suggest consulting your network and then interviewing at least three lawyers before selecting one. They can walk you through the components of the LOI, which I've outlined below.

INTRODUCTION

Your LOI to buy the company is your formal offer for the acquisition and serves not only as the preliminary agreement between buyer and seller, but also as the framework for the eventual deal and a road map for the negotiations ahead. M&A veterans will tell you that LOIs used to be no more than one to two pages, with just valuation and basic terms, but now, they are often six to ten pages or more, almost like a miniature purchase agreement.

When beginning the document, which often starts out looking like a letter but then turns into a term sheet, I suggest starting off with a personal note. Provide a heartfelt explanation of why you are excited about the potential acquisition and why you are the right person to carry on the legacy of the company—something that is a near-universal priority for sellers.

BASIC DEAL STRUCTURE

After your opening pleasantries, get down to business by clearly specifying the parties to the transaction, including the entity through which you will purchase the company, likely the name of the limited liability company (LLC) that will "hold" the company (versus you as an individual). After defining these entities, describe the type of transaction and how the deal will be structured. Common deal structure and terms include the following:

- **Stock purchase:** A stock purchase involves buying the company's stock directly, which means acquiring the entire business, including its operations, assets, and liabilities.
- **Asset purchase:** An asset purchase refers to acquiring selected assets and liabilities of the business—such as physical assets, intellectual property, and customer or referral lists—while typically excluding unwanted liabilities.
- **Full versus partial buyout:** In a full buyout, the buyer acquires 100 percent of the company. In a partial buyout, the buyer acquires a majority or minority stake, with the seller typically retaining some ownership through rollover equity.
- **Rollover equity:** Rollover equity is the portion of ownership that the seller retains after closing, which reduces the amount of capital the buyer needs to raise from outside sources.

Payment structure: Acquisitions can be financed in various ways. Buyers may pay in cash up front, defer payments through seller financing, or tie part of the price to future performance via an earnout. Rollover equity lets sellers retain a stake, while debt financing (loans) and equity financing (investor capital) help buyers reduce up-front costs.

Purchase price adjustments: These caveats help ensure a fair valuation by accounting for factors such as working capital adjustments, escrows and holdbacks (to cover postclosing risks), and indemnification provisions (to protect the buyer from undisclosed liabilities).

TARGET VALUATION

Next, you will lay out your proposed purchase price and payment terms. Naturally, upon receiving this LOI, the seller's eye will go straight to the money piece: the purchase price or, more accurately, the valuation of the company. In the LOI, this valuation is expressed as the **enterprise value**, which is the starting point for negotiating the final **purchase price**. For transparency's sake, I recommend you provide a brief description of how you arrived at that valuation. Not only does this reveal a thoughtful, data-driven process on your part; it also gives a more objective set of variables on which to base negotiations than if you simply proposed an arbitrary number. But how do you get there?

There are some widely accepted formulas to help you calculate the value of a business. One common approach for calculating a valuation is to use a multiplier of the company's EBITDA for the most recent year (often referred to as **TTM, trailing twelve months**). For example, for a company with $2 million in EBITDA in an industry where a 4× (pronounced "four times") multiple is common, the valuation would be $8 million. When valuing a business, the EBITDA multiple is highly industry-specific and fluctuates based on market conditions, growth potential, and risk factors. While a general starting point for many SMBs is 3–5× EBITDA, you should research industry comps for similar-sized businesses to ensure an accurate valuation. Of course, the EBITDA number itself is subject to diligence—note this accordingly or simply express the proposed purchase price as an EBITDA or revenue multiple instead of actual dollars.

Another accepted way to present a business acquisition valuation is through a revenue multiple. This approach is commonly used in early-stage or high-growth companies, where the earnings may not entirely reflect the potential value. Use caution here because, except for special circumstances, this could indicate a company that is not yet mature or profitable. Regardless, the concept is the same as an EBITDA multiple, in that you determine a multiplier to apply to the company's TTM revenue. Understandably, the common range of revenue multiples is lower, often coming in between 0.5× and 3×.

All that said, valuation can vary according to industry. When valuing subscription-based or software as a service companies with significant recurring revenue, the "Rule of 40" can be applied to determine if the company is sustainably balancing growth and profitability. According to this guideline, the combination of the year-over-year percentage increase in revenue plus the EBITDA as a percentage of total revenue—also known as the EBITDA margin—should equal or exceed forty. Businesses that score forty or above are generally considered to be financially efficient, and these more attractive investments will thus command a higher valuation multiple.

In addition to the quantitative equation, qualitative factors can also drive the valuation multiple up or down, including the overall size of the company, the growth rate, whether it generates one-time or recurring revenue, industry benchmarks, and the market trajectory. While it can be challenging to find comparable multiples for small businesses, you can often find sale multiples published online by brokerages. A quick tip to get you started: Search for the phrase, "XYZ industry valuation multiple," and drill down to find companies similar to your target in terms of size, business model, and financial performance. Likewise, don't hesitate to ask the seller's broker or banker what kind of multiples they are seeing in the market for similar businesses—not only will they educate you on the industry but they may also indicate the multiple the seller has in mind.

This brings me to another factor to consider—one that can be far less scientific and significantly more frustrating: the seller's expected price. In a perfect world, the seller has learned about the common valuation methods we have just reviewed and has researched valuation benchmarks and sale multiples of similar companies. Or, they have solicited input from experienced intermediaries and attorneys to appropriately set expectations. However, it's very possible that the seller is not familiar with market norms—or if aware, may believe their company's offering is unique or superior. In these cases, even if you can justify the numbers on paper, proceed with caution. If the seller perceives your valuation as unexpectedly low, you risk alienating them. It's akin to calling their baby ugly, and that alone may be enough for them to walk away.

PROPOSED FINANCING

Once you have a targeted valuation in mind, it is smart to run both the valuation and deal terms by any external financing partners you anticipate joining the deal, namely, your lender and lead investor. Taking this preliminary step will ensure that you have clarity on how much financing you can get and how much **debt service** the business can afford (the total cash a company needs to cover all debt obligations, including both loan principal and interest payments). Plus, preapproval on financing can strengthen your LOI and speed up the acquisition process. Be prepared to outline your proposed financing structure, indicating whether you will use debt, equity, or a combination of the two. Since most buyers will leverage some form of debt in a business acquisition, consider adding details of where you will solicit the funds (bank, SBA, mezzanine, etc.) and your confidence level in securing the needed amount.

When preparing for deal-specific conversations with your funding sources, have the business's financial statements and your projections ready for review. Also, be prepared to articulate why you are excited to acquire this company and your strategic plans for it going forward.

And don't limit yourself to just one bank—shop around for the best terms. Once you identify one or more debt partners that align with your investment thesis, ask them for a preapproval letter.

In addition to—or possibly instead of—using institutional debt, you can propose that the seller finance a portion of the deal through a **seller note**, in which you pay part of the purchase price over time rather than upfront, typically with interest. In this structure, the seller note would be subordinated to any institutional bank debt used in the transaction. As with traditional loans, seller financing includes formal debt documents and may require personal guarantees to ensure legal and financial clarity. Unlike institutional debt, however, the terms are negotiable. Most commonly, this includes the interest rate and repayment structure, which may involve interest-only payments for a period followed by a balloon payment at maturity.

Regardless of the details of the debt service, opting for a seller note benefits you, the buyer, by reducing the initial cash requirement and avoiding the need to shop around for favorable loan terms from banks. It also benefits the seller, offering them potential tax advantages and interest earnings, particularly if they are amenable to receiving less cash at the time of closing. The typical seller note covers between 10 and 30 percent of the purchase price, with some reports suggesting most fall in the 15 to 20 percent range.[14] However, depending on the situation, such seller financing can serve as the *sole* source of debt, especially if the seller prioritizes long-term benefits over immediate liquidity demands.

14 Kaitlinn Thatcher, "Understanding Seller Notes in M&A: Insights from 100 LOIs," *Axial*, last updated November 19, 2024, https://www.axial.net/forum/seller-notes-in-ma-data-insights-from-100-lois/.

PAYMENT STRUCTURE

Once you have outlined a specific valuation to include in your LOI, you should break down how the payment of the purchase price will be structured. The bulk of it will likely be cash at closing, but here is where you can offer creative options for paying the seller in other ways, including **rollover equity**, **seller earnout**, and a **forgivable seller note**.

First, how much of the business will be retained by the seller? You may assume it is zero, but often, this is not the case. Many sellers want a little **rollover equity**. In this scenario, you will purchase 100 percent of the company—but, at the time of closing, the seller will turn around and immediately invest a certain percentage of their proceeds back into the business. This amount can be whatever you both agree upon, but a typical range is anywhere between 5 and 20 percent, with 10 to 15 percent being the most common range in SMB acquisitions.

The seller's ongoing investment in the company they built aligns the buyer's and seller's interests and keeps the seller engaged in helping the company succeed. When the company is sold the next time, usually in three to seven years, the seller can cash out some or all of their retained ownership and get a "second bite of the apple," a widely used phrase to reference this later payout. This also minimizes the risk of the seller starting or joining an existing business in the same industry, in which they could leverage their deep knowledge and established network against you. Finally, rollover equity reduces the amount of financing you will need to raise from lenders and external investors.

If you need to give a little more but cannot stomach the thought of doling out more cash, two common approaches to paying a seller a portion of the proceeds over time include a **seller earnout**—future payments contingent upon the company's performance—and/or a **forgivable seller note**, which is a loan from the seller for a portion of the purchase price with interest rates and a repayment schedule.

A seller earnout is a common component of business acquisitions, often used when a seller is willing to defer a portion of the purchase price based on future performance metrics, such as profitability or revenue targets. This arrangement potentially boosts the final sale price for the seller while mitigating risk for the buyer, particularly if the seller's projected performance seems uncertain. However, earnouts can be complex and prone to disputes (it is sometimes said that "earnouts are lawsuits waiting to happen"), underscoring the necessity for sound legal guidance. Any metric for earnout performance measurement should be as objective and nonmanipulable as possible. Use well-defined, precise data points, such as revenue or gross profit, versus more subjective numbers that could be revved up or down, such as net operating income or margin. Note that some earnouts may not be permissible under SBA guidelines, so if you plan to get an SBA loan, be sure to consult your SBA lender and/or attorney.

Earnouts can be as simple (preferred) or as complicated as you want, as long as both parties agree on the terms and have clear definitions of data sources and triggers. Here is an example of how an earnout could be structured for a hypothetical home services business with $6.5 million in annual recurring revenue (ARR) and $1.2 million in EBITDA at acquisition, where the seller wants a $6 million purchase price (5× multiple), but you are only comfortable offering $5 million (just over a 4× multiple):

- The up-front payment will be $5 million, with a $1 million earnout over the next three years based on the following performance:
    - The seller will receive $500,000 if the business achieves $7 million in ARR by the end of year one.

- The seller will earn another $300,000 if the ARR grows to $7.5 million by the end of year two.
- The final $200,000 is contingent on the business reaching $8 million in ARR by the end of year three.
- If the revenue milestones are not met in any year, the corresponding portion of the earnout is either prorated or completely forfeited.

Another creative option for bridging a valuation gap—and maybe getting a good deal on debt in the process—is to use a forgivable seller note, also known as a forgivable promissory note. This approach combines the elements of a seller note (part of the purchase being funded through a loan from the seller) with an earnout, allowing for partial or complete forgiveness of debt if certain performance targets are not achieved. This structure provides considerable flexibility, including the ability for the seller to defer funds from the sale into different tax years while earning interest. This monthly paid interest is often attractive to the seller because it allows for continued monthly income after exiting the business.

A forgivable seller note can also serve as a risk mitigation tool. For instance, declines in revenue or the loss of key customers can trigger the forgiveness of portions of the note, keeping the seller engaged and somewhat accountable postclose. Again, there are constraints on these arrangements, such as SBA loan requirements mandating that the forgivable note be based on historical financials to avoid classification as an earnout. Typically, the forgivable seller note constitutes a smaller portion of the overall purchase price, around 10 to 20 percent.

FUTURE VISION

After describing your proposed valuation and deal structure for the transaction, you should share your vision for what will happen after the sale—namely, employee retention and seller transition. Not only will the seller want to know your intended fate of the employees and the management team, who are likely both colleagues and friends, but they will also take comfort in your commitment to keeping the company and its workforce stable during the transition. Detail any conditions you have for retaining the existing workforce with their current employment terms. If there are key personnel whose retention is crucial to the company's performance, consider adding a specific retention period, which often involves providing a retention bonus.

The other component of the workforce transition in an acquisition is what happens to the seller. How long will you want them to stick around? Do they want to retire and not look back or stay involved in a peripheral capacity, such as on the board? One of the more frequent tactics used here is to retain the seller in a consultative capacity on a contracted basis. Naturally, you will want to leverage the seller's expertise, network, and institutional knowledge to your advantage; however, be careful not to overcommit yourself to keep them employed. Although you may feel uncertain about operating the business, this will dissipate once you get on-site and start wrapping your head around the tasks at hand. I suggest keeping the initial seller's transition term short. Remember, you can always add to it—but once it is promised, it is hard to get out of, leaving you to pay the seller's retention fee or consulting rate for longer than you may like.

CAVEATS AND DISCLAIMERS

Then, there is the section with caveats and disclaimers. Your attorney will help you craft the appropriate language, but here are common factors to include:

- **Nonbinding nature:** Although the confidentiality and exclusivity sections (see below) are binding, the LOI is not a guarantee to proceed with the transaction.
- **Confidentiality:** All business discussions should be confidential, and the original NDA is often referenced in this section.
- **Exclusivity:** This is an important binding provision that allows you to prohibit the seller from engaging with other potential buyers while you are spending time and resources on pursuing the transaction. Binding exclusivity should be a minimum of sixty days but preferably closer to seventy-five to ninety days. This allows you to complete the most important parts of due diligence and get as close as possible to a signed purchase agreement before the seller can "shop the deal" with other prospective buyers.
- **Diligence plans and timelines:** You should give an overview of the diligence you expect to perform, noting any particularly relevant documents or information sources. Clearly state your expectation to have timely access to requested documents, personnel, and physical premises and that you may engage expert assistance to help you during the due diligence process. Wrap up this section with a high-level overview of the timeline for when diligence is expected to start and its expected duration.
- **Diligence and negotiation costs:** Specify who will pay for the expenses related to performing diligence on the company,

namely, the fees from professional services providers, such as attorneys and accountants. Typically, each party pays their own costs.

- **Specific conditions:** Outline the things that have to happen before you can close, such as securing financing, attaining regulatory approvals, and satisfactorily completing diligence.
- **Termination rights:** List the circumstances under which either party can terminate the negotiations, including any obligations or consequences arising from walking away, endearingly known as a "breakup fee."

A PERSONAL NOTE TO CONCLUDE

I like to wrap up an LOI with a personal note of gratitude and a reaffirmation of my interest, as well as a call to action on the seller's part, which includes a requested time frame for their response. It is customary to include an expiration of the offer contained within the LOI, mainly to ensure this phase does not drag on into perpetuity. Depending on the pace of the conversation up to this point, as well as what you have learned from the seller and intermediary regarding the desired timing, the deadline for your LOI could be as short as ten to fourteen days or take as long as thirty days. Be sure to include contact information for yourself or your representative if someone else will be handling communications on your behalf, such as an attorney or a buy-side advisor. End the document with signature blocks, including name, title, company, and date.

Trust and Integrity: The Cornerstone of a Successful Deal

Ideally, the seller reviews your LOI and promptly accepts it. If only it were that simple! The likelihood of the seller accepting your initial offer is quite low, and if they do, you have almost certainly offered too much. The more common scenario is for the seller to make a counteroffer, negotiating one or more of the terms you have proposed. Naturally, the most likely topic of consternation is the purchase price.

After reviewing the seller's objection(s) to the terms you have outlined, do your homework on the data points and market conditions surrounding the issue(s) at hand. Be prepared with relevant information to have a thoughtful discussion with the intermediary or seller about the elements under negotiation. Invite the seller to propose a counteroffer—and then you can bargain to resolve differences and move closer to an agreement.

While some negotiation on valuation is normal and expected, watch out for certain red flags during the process. For example, a seller might claim there's strong competition for the business to put you on the defensive—hoping you'll overbid or miss important details. Another red flag is the implication that you can bypass certain diligence items, such as QoE, because the business is too small or disorganized. Be wary if you are told that data is unavailable, as this could be a tactic to delay or obscure the transfer of unfavorable information.

As much as you can, make sure you maintain trust and integrity during the deal-making process, which is crucial for a successful outcome. Start by aligning your interests and values with those of the seller, ensuring a foundation of mutual understanding and respect. Communicate clearly, transparently, and frequently, keeping all parties informed and engaged throughout the process. Honor your commitments and adhere to agreed-upon timelines to demonstrate reliability and build confidence. Negotiate fairly and ethically, focusing on creating a win-win situation rather than seeking to exploit the other party. Finally, bring in key stakeholders and experts to ensure a well-rounded perspective and strengthen the credibility of the negotiations.

By following these principles, you can foster a sense of professionalism and respect in the deal-making environment. Once these talks play out, you can send over a finalized LOI with the agreed-upon terms. And then? It's time to celebrate. A signed LOI is a big milestone. Congratulations! Of course, that doesn't mean the work is done. The heavy lifting is in the diligence—and the next chapter gets into the details.

RN BOR

TURAL-

BORN

RAL-N

CHAPTER 6

DUE DILIGENCE

"You've got to know when to hold 'em, know when to fold 'em, know when to walk away, and know when to run."[15]

—"The Gambler," lyrics by Don Schlitz, performed by Kenny Rogers

Once you get a signed LOI, you are statistically more likely than not to close the deal. That is because the LOI, although nonbinding, represents a significant commitment—in time, resources, and emotions—from both parties. Again, it's like dating: Most people put years into a relationship before they put a ring on it!

That said, in life and in business, we don't always reach the altar. Personal and professional engagements alike get broken off—often for very good reasons. In the business world, diligence is how you might uncover a red flag worthy of "breaking off the engagement" post-LOI.

Due diligence is a rigorous and often tedious process that takes place after a price and deal structure are agreed upon but before the purchase is finalized. Every business has inherent risks, and the main objective is to identify any red flags that would give you pause or force

15 Don Schlitz, "The Gambler," performed by Kenny Rogers, United Artists, 1978.

your hand to call the deal off. Speaking of calling off a deal, do you know what your dealbreakers are? Pause right now and think about your target business; say out loud what would cause you to walk away completely. What are the two or three things that would make you stutter-step and go, "Wait, what?!" Until you know where your lines are, you will not recognize when one may have been crossed, especially when you are emotionally wrapped up in the deal.

In the best-case scenario, due diligence provides evidence for the stability of the business, uncovers opportunities for value creation, and helps reassure the buyer about potential returns. In the worst-case scenario, it can lead to renegotiating the deal based on findings or walking away from it altogether—a permanent breakup. This chapter explains the value of good diligence and provides an overview of the process and all it should include.

The Importance of Good Due Diligence

Due diligence is not an area where you want to skimp. Cutting corners here can be detrimental, as 70 percent of failed transactions are due to diligence-related issues, evenly split between QoE (Quality of Earnings) EBITDA discrepancies and non-QoE findings. We will talk more at the end of the chapter about ways a deal can go sideways. But for now, I want to focus on the value the process offers so you can see that it *is* worth your time, effort, and cost.

Before you wrote your LOI, you did your preliminary due diligence. Confirmatory due diligence, as the name suggests, involves verifying that everything communicated before the LOI, particularly financial and legal aspects, is accurate and true. For the general order of confirmatory due diligence, follow the FLO:

- **Financial:** Review the financials first because if those do not check out, you certainly will not want to waste time on the rest.
- **Legal:** Then, if the numbers work, you should meticulously comb through the company's legal documents and regulatory compliance metrics to ensure the revenue verified in the first step is both garnered legally and entirely transferable to you.
- **Operational:** The final bucket of work is the operational diligence, which likely runs concurrently with the first two steps and offers an opportunity to gauge both efficiency and effectiveness, as well as identify areas of value creation. Operational diligence offers a deeper dive into how the business operates. This phase should include interviews with customers, vendors, and employees—a prospect that makes sellers nervous. For many, this marks the first time they have disclosed to anyone outside of their innermost circle that they plan to divest of the business.

While very sensitive components may be withheld until just before or after closing, the bulk of the due diligence should be conducted thoroughly and promptly. Comprehensive due diligence in an acquisition is essential for several reasons. First, it ensures informed decision-making, as the insights gained can make or break the deal. Due diligence can identify potential risks and liabilities, which will hopefully help you mitigate risks that could otherwise negatively affect the transaction.

Due diligence can also be a way to sweeten the deal financially. Although you have already negotiated the purchase price, that number does not have to be final—if you discover something that devalues the business in the course of due diligence, you can return to the negotiating table. A thorough look under the hood allows you to get a clear and accurate valuation of the target company, much more than what you got during preliminary diligence, thus allowing for necessary adjustments to the purchase price. As a bonus, operational insights gained during this process are crucial for postacquisition integration and identifying strategic opportunities, which ensure a smoother transition and maximize the value of the acquisition.

According to *Harvard Business Review*, due diligence strives to answer four questions:[16]

1. **What are we *really* buying?** Until this point in the process, your understanding of the acquisition target has been primarily shaped by the mental image you have created from the offering materials and the commentary provided by the seller and broker. These optimistic data points naturally cast the target in a glowing light, which is what got you to the point of committing to pursuing the purchase. However, if you were to start from scratch and do the research yourself, would the narrative in your head be the same? This exercise includes personally completing industry and competitor research and authoring your own set of financial projections instead of relying on the seller's version.

2. **What is the target's stand-alone value?** The company must be able to financially stand on its own two feet, with all of the accounting tricks stripped out of the financial documents and without the benefit of future planned business synergies. It is commonplace for sellers to beef up financials in preparation for a sale in order to attract top dollar. This is not an overt attempt to cook the books but rather more like a new coat of paint and a landscaping upgrade on the house you are about to list. You should scratch off that topcoat and identify data points

16 Geoffrey Cullinan et al., "When to Walk Away from a Deal," *Harvard Business Review*, April 2004, https://hbr.org/2004/04/when-to-walk-away-from-a-deal.

that might not hold. Examples include jazzing up one-time sales in the hopes they will look recurrent, overestimating returns on recent new services or expenditures, or underfunding expenses to temporarily drive up EBITDA.

3. **Where are the synergies—and the skeletons in the closet?** In the *Harvard Business Review* article, synergies are discussed in the context of strategic buyers integrating a target into their existing business, but the same caution applies to owner-operators. You may believe you can drive growth through new sales channels or operational improvements, but as the article warns, overestimating synergies is a common pitfall. A disciplined buyer uses conservative assumptions about both the size of the gain and the likelihood of achieving it. The skeletons are just the opposite—hidden risks that can reduce performance after the deal closes, such as key employee turnover or customer loss.
4. **What is your walkaway price?** You should be consolidating everything you have learned in diligence to arrive at a definitive number: the maximum price you can justify paying for this business. This valuation is based on what is happening today, not at some point in the future or when certain synergies are attained. The authors suggest a practice of defending deal decisions with a slightly removed cohort of trusted advisors who will be more objective and unemotional.

Buying a business might sound glamorous—due diligence is anything but. This deal phase can take dozens of hours and tens or hundreds of thousands of dollars, making it tempting to perform only the rudimentary tasks and glaze over some of the harder questions.

This becomes especially true as the momentum of the deal grows and the desire to get closure (both from your emotions and the fatigue of the transaction itself) can cavalierly catapult you over speed bumps that would otherwise give you pause. Don't fall into this trap. I promise, as disruptive as it is to find out bad news during a diligence process, you will want to know now rather than later!

How to Begin the Confirmatory Diligence Process

Now that you understand why thorough due diligence is crucial, it's time to set your diligence goals. Write a list of data points you need to know inside and out, including details of financial statements, the terms of customer agreements and supplier contracts, and key operational metrics and ratios. Determine the biggest questions you want answered and define what discoveries would send you running for the hills. A good place to start is to think back on the questions you got from friends, colleagues, and mentors when you told them about this deal—make sure you can back up the reassurances you gave them with real numbers.

Once you know what you are looking for and why it is important, there are a few things that you will need before you begin the confirmatory diligence process:

- due diligence checklist and access to the data room (VDR)
- diligence providers in multiple areas of expertise
- funding for engaging diligence professionals
- reasonable expectations and a realistic timeline

Once you've clarified the goals of your diligence, the next step is to identify the specific data points needed to evaluate them and determine which documents or sources will provide that information. This is the basis of your **due diligence checklist**, which you will send to the seller and upload to the VDR. The broker will likely already have a data room set up. If not, you can do this yourself using free or low-cost document-sharing sites such as DocSend or ShareFile. Pro tip: Make sure the site administrator gives you permission in the settings to download the documents because you will want to work with the spreadsheets offline and send select information to your diligence providers.

While the seller's team is compiling and uploading these scores of documents—a process that will likely take two to four weeks—you should be coordinating the professionals who will help you formally evaluate your target. You want to find the right people, ensuring they are a good fit for your needs and available for the potential engagement. The myriad of diligence providers will vary based on industry, complexity, and size, but typical partners include the following:

- **Attorneys** to review contracts, assess risks, verify documents, and ensure compliance. Undoubtedly, legal fees will be your largest expense, but in almost every case, you get what you pay for. Seek out a transaction attorney with M&A experience, preferably within the industry of your target company.
- **Financial advisors**, which can include investment bankers, accountants, and financial consultants, who evaluate the financial health of the target company, including reviewing financial statements, assessing revenue streams, and analyzing projections.
- **Tax advisors**, who assess tax compliance and strategies, identify potential tax liabilities, and ensure that the acquisition structure is tax efficient. Sometimes your financial advisor can weigh in on tax matters, but M&A deals often require specialized tax expertise—so be sure to ask rather than assume.

- **Insurance advisors** to review existing insurance policies, identify coverage gaps, and evaluate risk management practices. If you are acquiring a founder- or family-led company, you may have to add directors and officers (D&O) coverage, particularly if you will have outside investors and/or a board. In every case, you should ensure that all insurance policies are transferable and will cover you on day one.
- **Operational experts**, who can evaluate the ins and outs of the target company's operation, including service adequacy, production processes, supply chain, and overall efficiency. These professionals may also be able to analyze market conditions, the competitive landscape, the customer base, and potential growth opportunities, or at least recommend an industry-specific commercial due diligence service or data source.
- **IT and cybersecurity advisors** to weigh in on the target company's IT infrastructure, data security measures, and potential vulnerabilities to cyber threats. If your insurance advisor recommends cybersecurity coverage, you may need to bring in an expert to assess which policy is most appropriate and whether the company's IT infrastructure can meet its requirements.
- **HR advisors** to review employment contracts, benefits, compensation structures, and organizational culture to discover any HR-related risks. They can also help identify key employees, assess potential turnover during the acquisition, and propose strategies for retention.
- **Regulatory and compliance experts**, who can ensure that the target company complies with industry-specific regulations and standards. This is particularly important if your business involves a licensed or regulated service, such as healthcare,

energy, financial services, telecommunications, food and beverage, or transportation and logistics.

Across the board, make sure you are consulting reputable professionals. This is *not* the time to save money by using your cousin who happens to be a CPA or your friend's father who is a retired law professor. With a qualified team to support you, you can complete the due diligence process with confidence.

DUE DILIGENCE CHECKLIST

Where do you find a customized checklist that aligns with your specific needs and industry requirements? Start by comparing your essential information requirements with standardized checklist templates available online, then adapt these templates by removing irrelevant items and incorporating questions that address unique aspects of the target industry.

I've summarized the most essential documents here. My website, lisapiercey.com, includes a complete due diligence checklist, which you can download for free.

A. ORGANIZATION AND GOOD STANDING

- The company's articles of incorporation and all amendments
- The company's organizational chart
- The company's list of shareholders and the number of shares held by each
- The company's minute book, including all minutes and resolutions of shareholders and directors, executive committees, and other governing groups

B. FINANCIAL INFORMATION

- Audited or reviewed financial statements for three years, including auditors' reports
- A schedule of accounts receivable
- A schedule of accounts payable
- The company's general ledger
- A schedule of inventory

C. PHYSICAL ASSETS

- A schedule of fixed assets and their locations
- All leases of equipment
- A schedule of sales and purchases of capital equipment during the last three years

D. REAL ESTATE

- A schedule of the company's business locations
- Copies of all real estate leases, deeds, mortgages, title policies, surveys, zoning approvals, variances, and/or use permits

E. INTELLECTUAL PROPERTY

- All intellectual property and data policies

F. EMPLOYEES AND EMPLOYEE BENEFITS

- A list of employees and independent contractors, including positions, current salaries, salaries and bonuses paid during the last three years, and years of service
- The company's personnel handbook and a schedule of all employee benefits and holiday, vacation, and sick leave policies

- A description of all employee actions within the last three years, including alleged wrongful termination, harassment, and discrimination
- A description of any labor disputes, requests for arbitration, or grievance procedures currently pending or settled within the last three years
- A list and description of the benefits of all employee health and welfare insurance policies or self-funded arrangements
- Verification of employees' professional certifications, especially for any roles that require licensing or formal credentials

G. LICENSES AND PERMITS

- Copies of any governmental licenses, permits, or consents
- Any correspondence or documents relating to any proceedings of any regulatory agency
- Records of compliance with information privacy regulations (such as the Health Insurance Portability and Accountability Act [HIPAA] in the US)
- Any data protection policies and compliance records (such as the General Data Protection Regulation [GDPR] for European customers)

H. ENVIRONMENTAL ISSUES

- Environmental audits, if any, for each property leased by the company
- A listing of hazardous substances used in the company's operations
- A list identifying and describing any environmental litigation or investigations

I. TAXES

- All tax and audit information

J. MATERIAL CONTRACT

- A schedule of all subsidiary, partnership, or joint venture relationships and obligations, with copies of all related agreements
- All loan agreements, bank financing arrangements, lines of credit, or promissory notes to which the company is a party
- All security agreements related to loans, collateral, or secured obligations (e.g., mortgages, pledges, or liens)
- Contracts with software vendors and any open-source software dependencies
- Agreements with partners or third-party service providers
- All other material contracts

K. PRODUCT OR SERVICE LINES

- A list of all existing products or services and products or services under development
- Copies of all correspondence and reports related to any regulatory approvals or disapprovals of the company's products or services

L. CUSTOMER INFORMATION

- A schedule of the company's twenty largest customers in terms of sales, and a description of sales over the last two years
- Any supply or service agreements
- The company's current advertising programs, marketing plans and budgets, and printed marketing materials

- A description of the company's major competitors
- Copies of all customer contracts and/or agreements

M. LITIGATION

- A schedule of all pending litigation
- A description of any threatened litigation
- Copies of insurance policies that possibly provide coverage for pending or threatened litigation
- Documents relating to any injunctions, consent decrees, or settlements to which the company is a party
- A list of unsatisfied judgments

N. INSURANCE COVERAGE

- A schedule and copies of the company's general liability, personal and real property, product liability, errors and omissions, key person, directors and officers, workers' compensation, cyber liability, and any other insurance contracts
- A schedule of the company's insurance claims history for the past three years

O. PROFESSIONALS

- A schedule of all law firms, accounting firms, consulting firms, and similar professionals engaged by the company during the past five years

P. IT AND CYBERSECURITY

- Cybersecurity audits, breach history, and incident response plans
- Data backup and disaster recovery plans

Q. ARTICLES AND PUBLICITY

- Copies of all articles and press releases relating to the company within the past three years

R. FUTURE STRATEGIES AND EXPANSION PLANS

- Any strategic planning documents or feasibility studies regarding future expansion
- Details on any planned new service offerings or technology deployments

Communicating Timelines and Scope

As you can see, the volume of information can quickly become overwhelming, so focus on being meticulously organized when managing the data room and handling documents. Speaking of overwhelming, you should anticipate the seller being taken aback by this long list of requested data. They will likely already have the basics pulled together, but many excited sellers will feel bogged down and even a little resentful of what can often feel like a screeching halt to the momentum of the process. The deal-making has been fun and exciting up until this point, but producing the requested diligence documents is decidedly a slog. So, while being patient and understanding, you should set a clear expectation of when the seller should have checked off most of the list.

Depending on the size and complexity of the deal, two to four weeks is usually a sufficient amount of time for the seller to upload the majority of the required documents. Feel free to start reviewing information as it comes in, but it is polite to hold your questions and additional requests until the checklist is substantially complete. Once the seller has indicated that they believe they have made a good faith effort to produce what you have asked for, return the favor by helping them understand your approach for completing a thorough analysis of the materials provided. While your LOI may outline a general timeline of the due diligence period, it's wise to clearly communicate your review schedule to the seller to ensure alignment on deadlines and expectations.

Once the seller has uploaded all necessary documents to the data room, beginning the due diligence process effectively involves a blend of thoroughness and efficiency. It is crucial to balance the depth of review with maintaining a swift pace to avoid frustrating the seller. Start by breaking down the due diligence tasks into distinct sections, prioritizing the areas that are most critical to the acquisition's success. Establish a clear timeline with specific target dates for completion of each segment of the review. Communicate this plan openly with the seller, explaining the significance of each phase—this transparency will not only help demystify the process for them but will also create accountability for you as the weeks tick by.

If issues arise or a deeper investigation is needed in certain areas, provide clear, reassuring explanations to the seller to keep communication lines open and maintain trust. Additionally, approach due diligence not just as a step toward closing the deal, but as a chance to uncover opportunities for improvement and long-term growth. This mindset helps ensure the process leads to a strong transaction and lays the groundwork for successful integration and postacquisition progress.

Questions to Ask During Due Diligence

When conducting due diligence, it's essential to categorize your efforts to ensure a thorough understanding of the acquisition's various aspects. Here, I've outlined some key questions in each category for you to answer as you review the requested documents. That said, please note that this is not a comprehensive list of *all* the questions you need to answer about the business you are buying. Beyond what's listed here, you need to seriously ask yourself—as well as industry experts and transaction advisors—what the specific rocks are that need turning over in order to get comfortable purchasing this company. This is *not* the time to cut corners or skimp on expenses! Thorough due diligence is crucial in uncovering both risks and opportunities, ultimately leading to well-informed decisions for you and your investors.

I've summarized the most essential questions here. You can find a complete list of questions, available as a free download, on my website.

DUE DILIGENCE QUESTIONS:

ORGANIZATIONAL FORMATION AND STRUCTURE

- What do the minutes from the company's meetings reveal about the decision-making process? Are the major decisions the company has faced in recent years adequately addressed?
- Does the organizational chart clearly define roles, responsibilities, and lines of reporting?
- Who are the primary shareholders, and what are the terms associated with their shares, including any options or warrants?

FINANCIAL INFORMATION

- Do the financial statements for the past three years raise any concerns about the financial health of the company? How do the recent unaudited financial statements compare to the previous years' audited ones?
- What does the cash flow situation look like? Are there any alarming cash burn rates?

- What are the main cost drivers and revenue streams? Are these sustainable?

PHYSICAL ASSETS AND REAL ESTATE

- What are the conditions, age, and locations of the company's fixed assets?
- What are the terms and conditions of the equipment leases?
- Where are the company's real estate properties located, and what are the terms of their leases or ownership?

INTELLECTUAL PROPERTY

- What intellectual property assets does the company own, and how are they protected?
- How does the company handle and protect its technical know-how and trade secrets?
- Are the company's software and data management practices adequate and legally compliant?

EMPLOYEES AND EMPLOYEE BENEFITS

- What are the terms of employment for key employees, and how likely is it that the transition will impact them? How dependent is the business on key employees, and what impact would their potential departure have?
- How comprehensive and competitive are the employee benefits, and what are the financial implications?
- What can you tell about the company's culture and morale from the employee turnover rates, educational training, and onboarding programs? What strategies are in place for employee retention, and what are the company's culture-building initiatives?

LICENSES AND PERMITS/ REGULATORY COMPLIANCE

- Are all necessary governmental licenses and permits current and compliant with regulatory requirements?
- Have there been any compliance issues, and how were they resolved?
- Are there industry-specific compliance requirements, and, if so, how does the company ensure compliance with these detailed regulations?

ENVIRONMENTAL ISSUES

- What environmental risks does the company face, and how are these being managed?
- Are there any pending or past environmental litigations or investigations?
- How does the company handle the disposal or management of hazardous substances?

TAXES

- Do any discrepancies or anomalies appear in the tax returns that could indicate financial or operational issues?
- Are there any ongoing or prior audits, and what were the findings of these audits?
- Are there any existing tax liens that could affect the assets or financial health of the company?

MATERIAL CONTRACTS

- What are the terms and conditions of critical contracts with subsidiaries, partners, and affiliates, and how do they impact the company?
- What dependencies or potential vulnerabilities arise from contracts with vendors or third-party service providers? How much vendor concentration exists, and what are the associated risks?
- Are there any risks associated with current loan agreements and financial obligations?

PRODUCT OR SERVICE LINES

- What is the current range of products or services, and are there any significant issues with them reported by customers? Are there any external tests or studies that can validate or give insight into the company's offered products or services?
- What are the trends in customer feedback, complaints, and warranty claims?
- What are the developmental stages and potential market impact of products or services under development?

CUSTOMER INFORMATION

- Who are the company's top customers, and how stable are these relationships?
- Are there any significant risks associated with customer concentration or issues with customer retention?
- What are the potential growth opportunities or risks identified in the marketing plans and customer contracts?

LITIGATION

- What litigation is currently pending, and what potential liabilities might it pose?
- Are there any significant past settlements or injunctions that could impact future operations or reputation?
- What is the coverage of insurance policies in relation to pending or potential litigation?
- How effectively does the company manage legal risks, and what does its history of disputes suggest about its operational practices?

INSURANCE COVERAGE

- What types of insurance coverage does the company maintain, and are they adequate for the nature and scope of its operations? Are there any gaps in coverage that could expose the company to uninsured risks?
- Is there a history of claims that could indicate underlying issues with the company's products, services, or operations?
- How are the premiums and terms of insurance likely to affect the company's ongoing costs and liabilities? Do any of your financing partners require you to add new coverage?

PROFESSIONALS

- What firms or professionals have been engaged by the company, and in what capacity?
- Is there continuity and reliability in the relationships with these providers?
- How do the qualifications and reputations of these professionals reflect on the company's standing and practices?

IT AND CYBERSECURITY

- Has the company experienced any significant cybersecurity breaches, and if so, how effectively were they handled?
- What are the current incident response plans, and how robust are they in addressing potential security breaches?
- How comprehensive are the data backup and disaster recovery plans? Are they tested regularly?

ARTICLES AND PUBLICITY

- What is the general tone and content of articles, press releases, and social media posts about the company? Are they predominantly positive, negative, or neutral?
- Have there been any significant public relations issues in the past three years that could affect the company's reputation?
- Does the company's online presence align with its stated values and mission?

FUTURE STRATEGIES AND EXPANSION PLANS

- What are the key elements of the company's strategic plan, particularly concerning market expansion and growth? Are there feasibility studies or market data that detail the expected outcomes of expansion efforts?
- What new service offerings or technology deployments are planned, and what strategic goals do they aim to achieve?
- How does the company plan to stay competitive in its market, and what innovations or changes are central to this strategy?

Download the full list of due diligence questions at lisapiercey.com.

As you seek the answers to these questions, please consider a second site visit during the diligence phase. Not only will you be able to ask more relevant and detailed questions than you did on your first visit, but there will also be a wealth of other data points you can pick up on simply from listening to the seller (often passionately) describing their business. At this follow-up meeting, you are likely to get access to additional key members of the leadership team, since the acquisition process is more advanced than it was on your last visit. It is hard to overstate the importance of these in-person conversations—they tend to reveal what really matters in the business, which can be crucial in steering your own due diligence efforts.

What to Do When You Encounter Adverse Findings

Let me tell you what a business acquisition is *not*: It is not a smooth, linear trek to a successful finish line. I could make analogies to roller coasters and curvy roads. If you're lucky, you'll only have one or two swerves, so you can get the deal back on track, hopefully without too much bad blood between you and the seller. The drama can be draining, with all the emotions to go along with it—especially if you turn over a rock during due diligence and find a snake underneath it.

What do you do if you discover an adverse finding during due diligence? Before you attempt to assess the impact of the finding, make sure you know all of the details. Let's be honest—the seller may not want you to know about the finding at all. They may not be trying to intentionally deceive you but rather attempting to glaze over it because it is resolved or no longer an issue. Or, it could be a current problem that they believe they can "fix" before closing and do not want to spook you during the transaction process. Alternately, they may have disclosed the issue but withheld vital details that convey its severity—for example, what is documented as a "cordial site visit by regulators" could actually have been an FBI raid. Trust your gut and ask questions. If something does not smell right, have a sit-down conversation with the seller, ask for documentation, and seek other sources or references.

Once you have the facts, or at least as much information as you can get, you will need to soberly evaluate the current and potential future ramifications of the issue. These can be financial, legal, operational, or reputational, and you may need the help of your team—accountants, lawyers, and consultants—to assist with the assessment. Once you definitively identify a problem, you should communicate that widely with all stakeholders.

While there are a host of ways that a deal can get off track, a handful of common themes tend to arise again and again. In a November 2023 Axial article, entitled "The Avoidable Mistakes That Derail Deals," the authors report that about half of small business exits fail because of missteps or inadequate preparation on the seller's part.[17] Watch out for the pitfalls they describe, such as

- lack of cleanliness and integrity of financials,
- no formal exit planning,
- caginess during due diligence,
- unfamiliarity with numbers,
- losing focus on business performance,
- running too narrow a process,
- not predefining the ideal outcome, and
- letting emotions cloud judgment.

---

17 Kaitlinn Thatcher, "The Avoidable Mistakes That Derail Deals," *Axial*, last updated November 16, 2023, https://www.axial.net/forum/the-avoidable-mistakes-that-derail-deals/.

On the whole, for these failed exits, 70 percent were because of an unfavorable due diligence finding, such as a QoE/EBITDA discrepancy (37.5 percent), a non-QoE diligence problem (35 percent), the seller electing not to proceed (12.5 percent), or an inability to secure financing (5 percent).[18]

If you do discover a material adverse finding during diligence, attempt to calculate the EBITDA impact. You can multiply the EBITDA change by the valuation multiple to come up with a starting place for a purchase price adjustment. For example, if you found a lost client contract worth $40,000/year in EBITDA during due diligence, when extrapolated out at a 5× multiple, you could argue for a $200,000 reduction in the purchase price. The key word here is *argue*, because even with solid evidence and easy math, any adjustment to the agreed-upon terms will entail serious discussion. Complicating matters is the fact that there are no hard-and-fast rules in retrading deals. Rather, it's just back to the negotiating table, but this time, under more time and cost pressures—and with the risk of disenchanting the seller at best and losing the deal altogether at worst.

Other remedies could be nonfinancial but equally as impactful. You could add legal indemnities and warranties to the purchase agreement to offset future risk, along with an escrow to hold funds to compensate for these potential problems. If the issue can be fixed with enough time, create a time-limited remediation plan with thresholds for moving forward while making sure you maintain exclusivity with the seller during this span of time.

An interesting arrangement for navigating a delayed closing, especially if the seller is ready to retire, is to offer to come in and run the business on a contract basis. They get some relief from running the business, while you get to finish your diligence from the inside and be

18 Thatcher, "The Avoidable Mistakes That Derail Deals."

part of the solution to the transaction's stumbling block. I used this avenue in a deal where a regulatory matter was holding up diligence—something neither the buyer nor the seller could influence or speed up. To salvage what could be a good deal, I negotiated an interim arrangement for me to operate the company as its contract CEO for a defined period of time, until the regulatory matter was resolved. The agreement allowed me to keep exclusivity on the acquisition during this time frame but still retain an option to walk away without penalty if desired. I ended up managing the company for several months before finalizing the purchase, which gave me the rare opportunity not only to finish my diligence from the inside of the company but also to get a head start on the learning curve of its operations.

While such workarounds can be effective, they are not always possible. In the end, if it is just too big of an issue to overcome, or if you and the seller can't negotiate an acceptable solution to the diligence finding, you have to walk away. It is a gut-wrenching decision that you will want to fight all the way because of the sunk resources and emotional costs. However, it's better than going full steam ahead with a bad deal. Know when to fold.

Once you do make this decision, consult with your legal and accounting teams to ensure you have met the proper conditions regarding notices and documentation. You may have some financial liability (the breakup fee) for terminating the deal, and there will be several notifications you will have to make. Above all, maintain professionalism and confidentiality despite your disappointment.

Fortunately, more often than not, due diligence confirms the deal is worth pursuing. When everything checks out and you're ready to move forward, it's time to formally wrap up the process and prepare for closing.

Wrapping Up the Process: The Due Diligence Summary

You have spent weeks—maybe even months—collecting, assessing, and integrating data. You are now positioned to present a much more accurate evaluation of the target's attractiveness, as well as its risks and potential pitfalls. Be aware of the emotional momentum you have built up, which is likely even stronger now that you have developed relationships with team members and have envisioned your future identity in this company. You may also feel pressure to complete the transaction because you have invested substantial amounts of time, energy, and thousands (if not tens or even hundreds of thousands) of dollars into pursuing this acquisition.

A best practice at this point is to compose a **due diligence summary**—an internal-facing document that captures the detailed findings uncovered during the diligence process. It's designed to highlight key risks, validate assumptions, and flag any unresolved issues before closing. This summary is often kept on file as part of the deal documentation, serving as a reference point for investors to evaluate how initial assumptions have held up over time and to inform future decisions. The document consolidates key findings such as the following:

- **Financial performance:** Summarize profitability, cash flow, and revenue stability, and note any concerns about the target's financial health and accounting practices.
- **Legal and regulatory compliance:** Document past, present, and potential future issues involving legal matters, intellectual property concerns, and compliance with regulations.
- **Operational efficiency:** Lay out the processes involved in the business model, including key inputs to its supply chain,

technology, and employee productivity. Identify promising opportunities for growth and synergies, in both the short and longer terms.

- **Competitive landscape:** Explain the company's market position, and describe its customer base and competitive advantages, highlighting relevant industry trends.

To conclude, make your recommendation on how to proceed—as planned but with conditions or contingencies, with a change in valuation, or with a thoughtful process for walking away. Once this summary is completed and agreed upon by any partners or trusted advisors, send your report, plus any supporting documentation (QoE, legal diligence memo, etc.), to your investors and lender. I recommend scheduling a follow-up virtual meeting to provide additional details, add anecdotes, and answer specific questions; this can be accomplished individually or in a group setting with all or most investors present and interacting with one another. Being transparent now will minimize surprises later, so communicate thoroughly.

Due diligence is an arduous process—you will feel like you are running the gauntlet, but it is worth every minute of effort. An ounce of discomfort now equals a pound of cleanup later! Now that you've made it through negotiation and due diligence, you're on to the next big piece of the puzzle: figuring out how to pay for the company you've just agreed to buy. It's a complex step but a critical part of bringing the deal to life. The next chapter gets into the dollars and cents.

RN BOR
TURAL-
BORN
RAL-N

CHAPTER 7

TYPES OF FINANCING

"You must take risks, both with your own money and with borrowed money. Risk taking is essential to business growth."[19]

—J. Paul Getty

Unless you are sitting on a pile of cash and can pay the acquisition cost and fees outright, you will need to pursue financing to buy your target company, likely through a combination of debt and equity—the two primary avenues for financing. In simple terms, **debt financing** is money that you borrow, with interest, to pay for a portion of the acquisition cost, and **equity financing** is funding that comes from external investors in exchange for an ownership stake in the company. Debt financing is the result of a loan process through a bank, private credit agency, or individual (most commonly the seller), while equity financing is generated from selling shares of the company to **high net worh (HNW) individuals** and/or **institutional investors**, such as a family office or PE fund.

---

19 J. Paul Getty, *How to Be Rich* (New York: Jove Books, 1965).

Most transactions will include both types of financing, and the ratio of each is driven by the company's stage of development, financial stability, industry characteristics, growth trajectory, and risk tolerance. A mix of the two is often used to balance the risks and rewards of each and optimize what is known as the company's **capital stack**—the breakdown of the different sources of money used to fund an investment. Even if you could self-finance the entire deal, you should consider bringing on at least some debt in order to boost returns—more on this later.

It is imperative that you educate yourself about your financing options to determine which one is best for this unique deal, while also keeping an open mind to all possible options. I say this because there are external circumstances that can influence your situation at any given time. I experienced this firsthand, as I've had to pivot my financing preference because of forces beyond my control.

In early 2023, I launched debt financing for one of my acquisitions during the same week of the Silicon Valley Bank collapse—the kind of event that tends to not only make investors and entrepreneurs nervous but also typically results in a more cautious banking environment, including tighter credit conditions. Talk about bad timing!

After pitching to literally a dozen lenders, I got two term sheets: one for a conventional loan at 9 percent interest, and one from a private credit fund at 14 percent interest. As counterintuitive as it might seem, I jumped at the latter opportunity. While the high interest rate did give me sticker shock, that option had other benefits: The private credit fund brought in a substantial chunk of equity, and the nonamortizing structure meant I only had to make interest payments (less than half of a normal monthly principal plus interest payment). The extra cash supported my plans for rapid operational expansion during the early years of the **holding period**—the length of time that I expected to retain ownership of the acquisition.

This underscores a simple truth: Context matters when you're talking financing. So, whatever route you may be considering now, take the time to educate yourself about *all* your options—and stay open to opportunities, which are often shaped by the larger economic landscape and competitive dynamics within the market.

Debt Financing Versus Equity Financing

Before we get into the types and sources of funding for a deal, compare the advantages and disadvantages of debt versus equity financing for *your* specific target company. I've broken down the pros and cons in a table, considering four key factors:

- **Financial obligation:** Debt creates an obligation of repayment, along with additional interest, whereas equity does not.
- **Impact on control:** Debt has no impact on ownership or control, but equity investors can exert significant influence based on their proportional stake.
- **Cost of capital:** After profit-sharing and dilution, the total cost of equity financing can far outweigh the cost of debt, with its fixed, predictable, and time-limited commitment.
- **Risk:** Equity financing spreads risk out across all investors, whereas debt puts financial pressure squarely on the company and its owner.

	DEBT FINANCING	EQUITY FINANCING
PROS	No dilution of ownership: You do not have to give up any shares in the company, and ownership remains unchanged. Predictability: You know exactly what is owed (principal plus interest, or maybe interest only for a while) and when it is expected. Time-limited nature: Once the note is paid off, you have no future obligation to the lender. Tax benefits: Interest payments are tax-deductible, which helps offset the cost of borrowing.	No repayment obligation: Equity is not repaid during the holding period, and if the business fails, there is no legal obligation to return the investors' initial capital. No interest payments: There are no periodic interest payments, which relieves pressure on the company's cash flow. Risk sharing: Investors' capital can provide a cushion during downturns, along with a potential willingness to offer additional **follow-on capital** for operating or M&A needs. Expertise and connections: Most equity investors are successful professionals, bringing with them industry knowledge, networks, and experiences that can boost your business.
CONS	Required creditworthiness: The lender will require proof that the company is on solid financial footing and has sufficient collateral, which could be tricky for some businesses. Pressure on cash flow: You are legally obligated to pay on a fixed schedule, regardless of your business's performance. Interest costs: Having to pay back interest on top of the borrowed principal can add significant costs to the deal, especially in an unfavorable rate environment. Risk of over-leveraging: Excessive debt puts the company, and perhaps you personally, at risk of bankruptcy if the cash flow cannot meet debt requirements.	Ownership dilution: Selling shares to external investors reduces your ownership stake and possibly your decision-making power. Potential for conflict: An investor or group with a large ownership percentage will have an outsized voice in business decisions, which could put them at odds with your preferences. Profit sharing: The upside of your company's performance must be shared with your investors, thus reducing your overall return. Exit expectations: The investors' expectation of a return on their investment could carry a different timeline or goals than what you had in mind for an exit strategy.

Figure 7.1: Comparing the pros and cons of debt versus equity financing.

Deciding on the balance between debt and equity financing involves assessing various factors related to your company's current situation, financial health, and strategic goals, as well as the overall market environment. When designing your capital stack, consider your planned strategies for value creation after acquisition. Are you going to need capital for growth to open new locations, enter new markets, or buy more equipment—or can you use operational cash flow to create value by upselling current customers or raising prices? In short, your capital structure drives your strategy and vice versa.

Financing a business acquisition is seldom an either/or choice when it comes to debt and equity—it is generally a both/and proposition. There is no magic ratio of debt to equity in an acquisition. While maximizing debt is usually preferred to boost returns, it carries risks and obligations that must be thoroughly assessed by both you and your external stakeholders. When evaluating debt, you must consider whether the company's balance sheet can absorb additional leverage (by which I mean debt) and whether its cash flow provides enough support to service the debt. Additionally, as with any loan, you must be comfortable with the market conditions, including the interest rate environment and your industry's expected headwinds and tailwinds.

DETERMINING HOW MUCH LEVERAGE TO USE IN AN ACQUISITION

When determining how much leverage (debt) to use in your acquisition, your biggest constraint may be how much the bank and/or seller will actually lend you. In some cases, particularly with SBA loans, you can borrow up to 90 percent of the purchase price—but should you? After all, the buck literally stops with you: You will be the one ultimately responsible for paying off the debt, and in instances where you have provided a **personal guarantee**, the assets that you and your family own can be seized to offset the loan balance if you default. This is how people lose their homes and their nest eggs. So, this decision is serious business and should be approached cautiously.

Although it can vary by industry, a typical starting point for an acquisition's debt-to-equity ratio is fifty-fifty or sixty-forty. When considering your debt-to-equity ratio, it's critical to consider the company's unique ability to service its debt. Thus, it's helpful to familiarize yourself with the objective calculations widely used by lenders to benchmark the amount of debt financing deployed in an acquisition:

- **Leverage ratio (debt-to-EBITDA):** This is a key metric in determining a company's ability to manage debt relative to earnings. It's calculated by dividing the business's total debt by its EBITDA. For a small business acquisition, a typically accepted range is between 2.0 and 3.0. Below 2.0 (two turns of EBITDA), your capital stack may not be fully optimized to produce growth or a return on equity. Above 3.0, you may have difficulty servicing debt if there is a downturn in earnings.
- **Debt service coverage ratio (DSCR):** This ratio reveals the business's capacity to cover its debt service (principal plus interest payments) with its operating income. It is calculated by dividing the EBIT (earnings before interest and taxes) by your estimated loan payments. A DSCR of 1.0 means you make just enough money to cover your debt payment—but of course, you will want some cushion for both growth and safety margins. In small business acquisitions, an ideal debt service coverage ratio should be a minimum of 1.2 and preferably closer to 1.5 or more to account for downturns.

Example: For a business with $1.5 million in EBIT and a purchase price of $8 million, the bank is offering you a five-year loan with a 9.5

percent interest rate. If you are targeting a DSCR of 1.3, you could support around $4 million in debt on the $8 million deal (fifty-fifty debt and equity split), which breaks down to an annual debt service in the first year of around $1.18 million.

DECIDING HOW TO STRUCTURE YOUR CAPITAL STACK

Ultimately, making the right choice for financing your acquisition involves a balanced consideration of all of the above factors, often with the assistance of financial advisors and potential lenders to analyze the specific implications for your business. At the end of the day, the decision should align with both your personal philosophy toward debt as well as your long-term business goals and the financial health of the company.

Now that you have an idea of how you want to structure your capital stack, let's consider the specific sources of debt and equity—and talk about tactics to help you get what you need for your acquisition.

Sources of Debt Financing

When considering debt financing, it is important to identify the most advantageous source(s) for your situation. SBA loans are one of the most common forms of debt financing for small business acquisitions, often sought because of their favorable terms and accessibility. Conventional bank loans and seller financing are also commonly used, which can help bridge gaps in funding. When additional capital is needed and traditional options are limited, mezzanine debt or convertible notes may be used to complete the capital stack.

SBA 7(A) LOANS

The SBA is a government agency that offers multiple financing options, with the 7(a) loan program being its most popular. Another commonly referenced SBA product is its 504 loan, which is geared toward financing real estate and fixed assets. While a 504 loan can be used in business acquisitions involving significant real estate and/or equipment purchases, it's a less versatile tool—which is why I focus on the SBA 7(a) loan program here.

For first-time buyers, SBA 7(a) loans are a popular option, with many SBA-approved lenders specializing in business acquisitions. From a creditworthiness standpoint, your likelihood of approval increases if you are experienced in the industry and are already in the market, acting as an owner/operator. It's crucial to engage with a banker before issuing an LOI to ensure the deal is structured in a way that is financeable. While these loans are initially highly leveraged, it's common for buyers to refinance with a conventional loan after four to five years, potentially removing the personal guarantee.

Pros:

- High leverage: The SBA 7(a) program allows buyers to finance up to 90 percent of the enterprise value of the business. This level of leverage is higher than what is typically available with conventional loans, which generally cap borrowing at around 50 percent of the purchase price.
- No financial covenants: Unlike conventional loans, SBA 7(a) loans do not have restrictive covenants that require the business to maintain specific financial ratios, such as maximum leverage or cash flow requirements.

- Longer amortization period: Most SBA 7(a) loans offer a ten-year term, double the usual five years for conventional loans.
- Access to capital for first-time buyers: For business acquisitions, the SBA encourages banks to provide financing for ventures that might otherwise be considered too risky by guaranteeing a significant portion of the loan. The high leverage is also a plus for first-time buyers without a lot of capital.
- Only requires a 10 percent equity injection from the borrower (you, the buyer), significantly less than conventional loans. Buyers must contribute at least 5 percent in personal funds, with the remaining 5 percent allowed to come from a seller note on full standby for the life of the loan.
- Option to refinance after four to five years.
- No prepayment penalties on a standard ten-year SBA 7(a) loan.

Cons:

- Personal guarantee required: These loans require a personal guarantee from any owner with more than a 20 percent stake in the business, which may include pledging personal real estate as collateral.
- Higher fees compared to conventional loans.
- Lengthy approval process.
- Limited to businesses with enduring profitability.
- Upper loan limit of $5 million.

SELLER FINANCING

With seller financing, the seller provides a loan to the buyer to cover a portion of the purchase price. Typically, a seller note can finance up to 50 percent of the acquisition, and possibly more, although it is generally not used to cover the entire amount. To refresh: A seller note is a form of financing used in small company sale transactions in which a seller agrees to receive a portion of the acquisition proceeds in a series of debt payments. This arrangement allows the buyer to bridge a funding gap without needing to secure the full amount from traditional lenders or equity investors.

To "sell" this arrangement to the seller, remind the seller that the note will provide them with ongoing income through the payments made over a term of five to seven years. This "mailbox money" helps the seller gently wean off his/her former salary, thus easing the transition. It can also offer favorable tax implications for the seller, as the income is spread out over time rather than being taxed as a lump sum.

Pros:

- Faster than third-party financing: Because the seller already knows the business well, the due diligence process is quicker and easier.
- Flexible: The seller can set their desired interest rate and terms (should be competitive with market rates or at least close).
- More efficient: This arrangement benefits both parties by making the acquisition process smoother and faster. Seller financing can be a valuable tool to close the deal, especially when traditional lending options fall short.

Cons:

- May require a personal guarantee: The seller may check your credit score and secure the loan with the business's assets or cash flow as collateral and request that you sign a personal guarantee to ensure repayment.

CONVENTIONAL LOANS

Conventional loans are those issued by a traditional lender such as a bank. When considering a conventional loan to finance a small business acquisition, be prepared to meet the bank's key requirements, which can sometimes feel intrusive and over-the-top. Lenders typically demand that you have a strong credit score, a solid financial history, and adequate collateral, which could include both business and personal assets.

The process of securing a conventional loan can be time-consuming, given the in-depth diligence to be completed by the lender. This type of financing is less flexible than seller financing or SBA 7(a) loans, which often allow for more lenient terms and quicker approvals. However, if you meet the qualifications, a conventional loan can be a solid option for funding your business acquisition, providing market-based rates and straightforward repayment terms as long as you can maintain the conditions and requirements.

Pros:

- Competitive interest rates: Conventional loans typically offer competitive interest rates and shorter repayment terms, allowing you to pay off the loan faster and reduce long-term interest costs.

- Access to a revolving line of credit: A traditional bank can also provide you with a revolving line of credit (**RLOC or revolver**) to be on standby after closing the deal. When negotiating your term sheet, consider including a revolver, especially if the business has high working capital requirements. Even if you think you might not need it, an RLOC can be a valuable and comforting backup plan, as there is no interest expense unless you use the available funds.

Cons:

- High down payments: You will be expected to make a down payment of up to 30 percent of the purchase price.
- Little wiggle room: Shorter repayment terms mean higher monthly payments, without much flexibility.
- Stringent financial covenants: The lender will likely require you to adhere to financial covenants, such as maintaining specific financial ratios and restricting borrowing from other sources.

MEZZANINE FINANCING

Mezzanine financing is a hybrid form of funding that combines elements of both debt and equity, making it a useful tool in business acquisitions. Just as the mezzanine level in a building serves as a bridge between floors, mezzanine financing bridges the gap in the capital stack, typically between **senior debt** (borrowed money that a company must repay first if it goes out of business) and the equity you have raised.

This type of financing is particularly valuable when you need additional capital, but your primary lender is maxed out and you still have a modest equity gap. Mezzanine debt is a form of **private**

credit, which is an increasingly popular category of nonbank lending provided by institutional investors, as it can be tailored to the specific needs of a private company, such as acquisition, growth, or restructuring. The flexibility of mezzanine financing allows the debt to be structured to fit the needs of your acquisition, often with terms that can be customized to your specific situation. For small business acquisitions, typical providers of mezzanine financing include dedicated private credit funds, PE funds, and family offices, although you can occasionally source it through banks and credit unions.

Pros:

- Possibility for a nonamortizing loan: One of the key features of "mezz debt" is that the loan is often **nonamortizing**, meaning you will only be required to make interest payments during the term of the loan, with the principal due at maturity.
- Can include an equity component: This makes mezzanine financing technically a hybrid of traditional debt and equity financing. The equity component of mezzanine financing typically involves either a straight equity contribution or, more often, an equity-like instrument, such as **warrants or options**, which are financial tools that give the holder the right, but not the obligation, to purchase equity at a predetermined price within a specific time frame, usually at exit.
- Aligned lender interests: Regardless of the specific components, a lender's participation on both sides of the capital structure aligns their interests with the growth and success of the business, since they will be sharing in the upside. In addition, while there is no guarantee, this dual play of holding both debt and equity securities makes for more "patient

capital," with less likelihood that the lender will quickly default your loan if you run into temporary troubles.
- Potential for strategic guidance: Mezzanine lenders may bring helpful industry expertise to the table, providing not just capital but also strategic input. Because of their significant investment, these lenders often seek a board seat to influence key business decisions, ensuring that the company's direction aligns with their interests and the overall success of the acquisition.

Cons:

- High interest rates: The interest rates for mezzanine debt are almost always noticeably higher than other sources of debt, usually 12 to 14 percent compared to 6 to 9 percent at the time of this writing. This reflects the higher risk the lender assumes by subordinating to senior debt in the capital stack.
- Strategic guidance comes with a price: While a mezzanine lender's multifaceted engagement is appealing and often helpful on many levels, you can pay the price of feeling more like the beholden CEO of a PE fund portfolio company than an owner/operator of a small business.

CONVERTIBLE NOTE

Another blended debt and equity security is the convertible note, which is a type of short-term debt that converts into equity in the company, typically at a future financing round, upon the achievement of certain milestones, or at exit. This means that instead of being repaid in cash, the lender or investor receives shares of the company (equity) at a predetermined conversion rate, which is sometimes discounted from the cost per share of other investors in order to sweeten the deal. Like other debt sources, convertible notes carry an interest rate, which can be paid off throughout the term or can be accumulated for **payment-in-kind** and converted to equity shares at maturity.

Like mezzanine financing in a small business acquisition, a convertible note can be used to bridge the gap between the buyer's available capital and the total purchase price. Typical sources of convertible notes are HNW individuals, angel investors, VC firms, and PE funds; seller financing can even include the use of a convertible note.

Pros:

- Mutual flexibility: Convertible notes offer flexibility for both the buyer and the lender. For you, the buyer, it provides a flexible financing solution and reduces the amount of traditional debt or equity you must raise for the acquisition. For the lender, it provides the opportunity to convert their participation into equity and take advantage of the upside created through the value you bring.
- **Aligned incentives:** Since the lender has the option to convert the note into equity, they're often more invested in the long-term success of the business rather than just short-term repayment. This encourages a more collaborative relationship, where the lender may offer support, connections, or strategic input to help the business grow—knowing they could share in the benefit if things go well.

Cons:

- **Structural complexity:** While convertible notes are common in start-up and venture deals, they can be unfamiliar or confusing in small business acquisitions—especially for sellers or lenders who aren't used to hybrid instruments. If the terms around conversion aren't clearly defined or well understood, it can lead to miscommunication, legal complexity, or friction down the line when the note is triggered.

- **Ownership dilution and cash flow pressure:** If the lender converts the note to equity, your ownership stake could shrink—especially if the business grows before conversion. This can affect control and future fundraising. Also, if you choose to pay interest during the holding period, it can create cash flow pressure during a critical phase of growth.

Financing Best Practices

While this chapter on financing follows the confirmatory due diligence section, your actual fundraising should not! As mentioned previously, you should first reach out to a lender as soon as you have identified a serious acquisition target and have conducted preliminary due diligence, preferably before submitting your LOI. This will help you get prequalified and may allow you to knock some initial tasks off the list before the transaction activity ramps up.

Certainly, the minute you get a signed LOI, get to work on fundraising! Tackling this gargantuan task early is crucial because it sets the stage for a smooth and timely closing process. Now that you have a clear understanding of the deal terms, the lender can begin their due diligence and underwriting process, thus reducing the risk of delays that could jeopardize the deal. Additionally, in a volatile market environment, starting the financing process right after LOI signing helps you lock in potentially favorable interest rates and terms before conditions change and gives you ample time to address any issues that may arise during the lender's review.

Now, with all that said ... What does the process of securing funding look like? The next chapter covers best practices in financing your deal.

RN BOR

TURAL-

BORN

RAL-N

CHAPTER 8

FINANCING THE DEAL

"No one ever made a decision because of a number. They need a story."[20]

—Daniel Kahneman

Just as there are different types of financing, there are different approaches to fundraising for your acquisition. I will be honest: The process can be tedious and time-consuming, with plenty of paperwork required. However, it's a worthy investment of your efforts—not only because of the potential for funding but also because of the relationships you may build as you go through it. Even if a financing pursuit doesn't take hold immediately, the connections you make may reap rewards later.

One of my most helpful (and favorite) equity holders is a professional investor with whom I connected through cold email outreach prior to an ACG event. My intern had reviewed the list of capital providers planning to attend the conference and identified this investor's firm as potentially being aligned. Along with a couple dozen other

20 Michael Lewis, *The Undoing Project: A Friendship That Changed Our Minds* (New York: W.W. Norton & Company, 2016), 250.

points of contact, I sent this gentleman the teaser for the independent sponsor deal for which I was currently fundraising. While he quickly disqualified the acquisition as being too small for his firm, he did express interest on a personal level and suggested we meet up at one of the event's social gatherings. Our conversation at that reception was the beginning of a new business relationship that resulted in me getting lots of great advice, thought-provoking questions, and a six-figure investment—and it all started with a cold email that cost me nothing to send.

So, as you approach people for financing, think of it as a relationship-building exercise, not a cash grab! The organization or person you're approaching might not be the right fit—but they might know another person or organization that is. Or they might be the right investor for another deal down the line. Who's to say this will be your only acquisition? As you navigate the fundraising process, keep the long game in mind.

Raising Debt Financing

In the previous chapter, I talked about the two buckets of financing, debt and equity, and the likelihood that you'll probably end up using both to fund your acquisition. The processes for raising debt financing versus raising equity financing are a bit different. Here are my recommendations for securing the debt you need for your deal:

- **Determine your needs:** Assess the amount of debt required by considering your leverage ratio, debt service coverage ratio, and cash flow expectations.
- **Prioritize financing options:** Based on your risk tolerance, financing goals, characteristics of the target company, and the current interest rate environment, rank your preferred debt financing options. In challenging economic conditions, be

prepared to combine different sources to reach your optimal funding level.

- **Prepare a strong pitch deck:** Ensure your pitch deck is comprehensive, including all relevant financial and performance data of the target company, along with your growth and value creation plans. Be ready to present and sell your vision multiple times.
- **Ensure personal financial health:** Make sure your own financial situation is solid, demonstrating your creditworthiness to potential lenders.
- **Leverage existing relationships:** Begin with lenders you know personally, drawing on relationships you've cultivated over time. If your contacts are not a good fit for this acquisition, ask them for introductions to other potential lenders.
- **Engage in multiple meetings:** Conduct numerous initial meetings, preferably face-to-face, and be prepared to provide additional follow-up information, including granting data room access when necessary.
- **Compare term sheets:** Collect multiple term sheets if possible, and compare them according to key parameters, such as interest rates, fees, and repayment flexibility to accommodate potential fluctuations in business performance.
- **Negotiate term sheets:** Term sheets aren't set in stone! While it is important to mind confidentiality (don't mention specific names or share actual documents), it is perfectly acceptable to compare term sheets from different lenders and use them as leverage in negotiations to secure the most favorable terms for your acquisition.
- **Review and finalize:** Before signing your preferred lender's term sheet, have it carefully reviewed by your financial advisor

and attorney, and give your lead equity investor the opportunity to review it and provide feedback.

In many small business acquisitions, you'll need to bring in outside capital to supplement your debt financing. Equity fundraising will almost certainly play a central role in that process. Chances are, you're unfamiliar or inexperienced with equity financing—and that's OK. Most people are. The rest of this chapter walks you through it.

Raising Equity Financing

While raising equity financing can be one of the most challenging aspects of an acquisition, it also offers unique rewards, as well as a fascinating look into how other people view the target company that you hold in such high regard. By engaging investors who share your vision, you not only secure the necessary capital but also gain valuable partners who can contribute to the growth and success of the business. Understanding the nuances of equity fundraising is essential for navigating this stressful, yet potentially transformative, phase of your acquisition. And you've got to navigate it well—because there isn't really a contingency plan if fundraising falls short. The deal dies, the seller gets annoyed, and the buyer loses credibility. In short: You want to get your fundraising right and avoid this worst-case scenario.

But first, we will start with a familiar equity source that should always be the acquisition's first investor—you. When funding a small business acquisition, most consider it essential for you, as the buyer, to invest some of your own capital to demonstrate commitment and show that you've got some skin in the game. This personal investment not only reinforces the buyer's confidence in the success of the acquisition but also reassures other financiers, such as lenders and equity investors, that the buyer is fully engaged in the outcome.

Do not be discouraged if you are not sitting on a six-figure pile of cash to plop down in the capital stack. Your own equity contribution can be much more modest while still being meaningful—and it can come from various sources. The most straightforward options include deploying cash savings or selling off liquid assets, such as stocks, ETFs, or cryptocurrency. Other sources include liquidating real estate holdings or responsibly tapping into retirement accounts through no- or low-penalty options such as a **Rollover as Business Start-ups (ROBS)**—a structure that allows buyers to use retirement funds to help finance a business acquisition without early withdrawal penalties or taxes. Other options lower on the list include leveraging your home equity through a home equity loan or line of credit, pursuing smaller dollar loans from friends and family, or crowdfunding. Regardless of the source of your personal equity contribution, participating as an equity investor in your own acquisition demonstrates commitment, fosters trust with other investors, and helps the deal move forward.

SELLER ROLLOVER

In addition to your own equity contribution, there is likely another "internal" investor in this deal that can be added to the **cap table** (**capitalization table**—a document detailing a company's ownership structure) before seeking external equity financing: the seller's rollover equity. This component was likely fleshed out in your LOI and negotiated earlier in the acquisition process. If it was not, it is worth asking the seller to be one of your equity investors. Since you and the seller have gotten to know each other better throughout the diligence process, they may be more willing to forgo some of their sale proceeds and reinvest in you and your future plans for the business.

Seller rollover can be thought of as retained equity, where the seller keeps a small portion of the business even after the sale. In other words, they "roll over" part of the money they receive from the sale and put it back in the deal as one of your equity investors. This strategy is widely referenced as the seller getting a second bite of the apple because the seller can receive a later payout upon a future liquidity event. The seller also has the advantage of deferring taxes on the rollover amount, since this amount is not paid out at closing but rather rolled into an ownership stake. Beyond the financial aspect, retaining a minority interest allows the seller to stay connected to the business they have built and been passionate about for years, minimizing the risk that they will feel irrelevant or left out of the loop. This can also provide reassurance to their customers, colleagues, and friends that they still believe in the company's future and are committed to its ongoing success.

For the buyer, the main advantage is that it reduces the amount of cash needed to finance the purchase. Additionally, it aligns the seller's interests with yours, keeping them engaged and (literally) invested in the success of the business, which can be particularly valuable both during the transition period and when facing future challenges. Likewise, other external investors will be reassured by the fact that the seller—who knows the business better than anyone—has confidence in you and the trajectory you have mapped out for the company.

Seller rollover equity is typically structured with the seller retaining 10 to 30 percent of the equity in the business. The terms of the rollover are negotiable and can be assigned as either preferred or common stock, with flexibility in liquidation preferences depending on what works best in your capital stack. At higher percentages of retained equity, it is important to consider whether you want the seller to maintain significant influence in the business, as they could become the lead investor or largest shareholder, which may or may not align with your vision for the company's future. In addition, the seller might have their own ideas about governance, value creation plans, and exit strategy, making it crucial to have a candid discussion about what their retained ownership means—and does not mean—for their future role in the company. This ensures clarity and alignment on both sides, preventing misunderstandings and potential conflicts down the road.

RAISING EXTERNAL CAPITAL FROM INVESTORS

This may be the section that stops you in your tracks. From your early days of school fundraisers to your recent service on a nonprofit board, you have probably felt uncomfortable asking people for money. Most people would rather write a check themselves than ask others for a donation. But remember how it was a little easier to raise money when you were able to give the donor something enticing in return? Folks are always happy to overpay for cookie dough or fruit boxes in support of their local sports team. Raising equity financing is no different! Not only do you have an attractive product offering—partial ownership in a thriving business—but, in most cases, the "wares you are hawking" will ultimately put more money back in the donor's pocket. And who wouldn't want that?! Undoubtedly, the prospect of equity fundraising is mysterious and intimidating to most, but it can be broken down into some fairly manageable and straightforward steps.

Setting Up Your Special Purpose Vehicle

Before you begin raising external capital, you should set up a **special purpose vehicle (SPV)**. In the US, an SPV, sometimes just called a vehicle, is often structured as an LLC, but there are situations where a C corporation, S corporation, or limited partnership might be more appropriate. This new legal entity will hold the new target company as a wholly owned subsidiary. The SPV will be the named entity on the acquisition documentation, bank accounts, and governance matters. It will provide clarity, keeping everything business-related separate from your personal matters, and will streamline the collection of equity contributions, limit liability for both the target company and you personally, and potentially offer tax benefits. In the future, the SPV will offer a "clean asset" to make your eventual exit more straightforward through the sale or transfer of the entire entity. If you have already raised search capital through a traditional search fund, you likely have already completed this step.

You will need input from both your accountant and your attorney to determine the optimal legal and tax structures for your SPV and for drafting its formation documents. However, there are several steps you can do yourself, saving on professional fees and expediting the process, such as registering with the Secretary of State in your chosen jurisdiction, obtaining an Employer Identification Number (EIN) from the IRS, and opening a bank account to hold and then disburse funds raised for the acquisition.

If you plan to get bank debt for the acquisition or a line of credit for your target company, you should plan on setting up your SPV account at the same bank. Having this account, along with your new company's deposit account(s), under the same roof as your debt not only wins you brownie points with the bankers and loan committee but is also often required for the loan. When selecting a bank, choose on the basis of relationships—banks will almost all have the same technical capabilities, but you want to be able to pick up the phone and call *your* banker with any concerns or needs. In my experience, regional or boutique banks are often a better fit for the needs of small business acquirers than large, national institutions.

Identifying Investor Leads

Where do you find people who want to wire you tens or hundreds of thousands of dollars for your acquisition? Your network, of course!

To successfully raise equity for a business acquisition, it is crucial to start building relationships well in advance of needing capital. Begin by reaching out to potential investors long before you are ready to present the deal—share your interests, discuss emerging opportunities, and ensure that your values align. This allows you to practice talking through deals you're considering, even if they're not yet under contract.

Remember, you will be working closely with these investors for the next five-plus years, interacting regularly and potentially navigating challenging situations together, so it is essential to genuinely like and trust them. Starting early also means that by the time you have a signed LOI, you have already had several conversations, gathered interest in the acquisition, and secured soft commitments. This way, when it is time to actually raise capital, you are not starting from scratch but rather calling in the commitments you have been nurturing all along.

If you find yourself without a robust list of well-resourced contacts, you will need to build one quickly. The old adage comes to mind: "The best time to plant a tree was yesterday, and the second-best time is today." Start making a list of everyone you know who might have any of these characteristics: business owner, inventor/innovator, entrepreneur, high-earning professional (physician, attorney, corporate manager, etc.), experienced investor, political or philanthropic donor, financial advisor, retired executive, or board member. In general, your initial list should have dozens, if not one hundred or more, names because you have to cast your line *a lot* of times to get even a few bites.

When identifying potential equity contributors who are investing individually and not through a fund, they must meet the criteria outlined by the Securities and Exchange Commission to be considered an **accredited investor**. To qualify as an accredited investor, an individual must have an annual income of at least $200,000 (or $300,000 combined if they have a spouse) for the last two years or a net worth exceeding $1 million, excluding their primary residence.

So, let us look at the five primary segments of investors in SMB acquisitions:

- **Friends and family** are often the first line of support for acquisition entrepreneurs, since they are usually willing to invest based on personal relationships and trust. These investments can be more flexible in the terms and expectations but can also carry emotional risks if the business does not succeed as planned.
- **High net worth (HNW) individuals**, sometimes called **angel investors**, are affluent individuals who provide capital for start-ups and small businesses in exchange for equity ownership. They often bring not only financial resources but also expertise, mentorship, and valuable connections to help the business grow.
- **Investor syndicates** are groups of individual investors who pool their resources to invest in a business. This allows smaller investors to participate in larger deals and spreads the risk among multiple parties. Syndicates are typically led by a more experienced investor or firm that manages the investment on behalf of the group.
- **Family offices** are private wealth management firms that manage investments for ultrawealthy families. These families often look for long-term investments and can provide significant capital. Family offices may be particularly interested in small business acquisitions if they align with the family's investment strategy or values.
- **Private equity funds** invest in businesses with the aim of increasing their value and eventually selling them for a profit.

They typically seek more substantial investments and usually want an active role in managing the business, typically via the board. PE funds are best suited to businesses with a strong growth appetite.

If your personal and extended network still does not render the denominator size needed, you might have some luck generating interest from strangers. While cold-calling potential sellers in the deal-sourcing phase is often considered a low-value proposition, reaching out to previously unknown investors in your equity fundraising stage can yield better results, especially in the SMB acquisition space. In the last decade or so, this asset class has begun attracting a niche set of HNW individuals and even institutional investors who have a genuine interest in small business investing. Many of these investors are connected to searchers or search funds, but your approach does not have to follow the traditional search fund model to capture their attention. Social media platforms such as X and LinkedIn have become valuable resources for finding these investors, thanks to the growing popularity of ETA, as seen in the rise of online groups and content dedicated to the topic. Additionally, databases of SMB investors are sometimes shared online or through social media, offering another avenue for identifying potential backers.

An efficient way to connect with investors is by attending "capital connection"–type conferences, such as the ACG event I mentioned in this chapter's introduction. These events are typically centered around lower middle market deals, including search funds and independent sponsors. By registering for these events, you often gain access to a list of attendees a few weeks beforehand, allowing you to proactively reach out to potentially aligned investors. Sending out your teaser before the conference can help you secure in-person meetings during the event and will give you a head start on networking. These conferences are prime hunting grounds for capital sources actively seeking investment opportunities, so your outreach is likely to be well received. Even if some institutional investors pass on your deal, they might be able to refer you to a better-suited fund, or the point of contact could even be interested in investing on a personal level! As a bonus, these events are also heavily attended by lenders and diligence providers, making them an excellent way to connect with multiple potential partners in a short period of time—helpful if you are in need of these services.

The Process of Asking for Investment

As with most things in life, success when pitching depends largely on preparation. Investors will expect you to know your target company inside and out. Be ready to present a clear and compelling narrative about the business and how it fits into your entrepreneurial journey. You will pitch this story many times, so make sure it resonates internally, whether it is about fulfilling a personal mission, developing yourself professionally, or preserving a legacy. Of course, it's not just about telling a nice story—you need data to back up your claims. That's where your investor materials come into play.

In some ways, asking for investor equity is more of an art than a science. However, there are three hard and fast rules worth following to increase your odds of success: present data-supported projections, prepare high-quality investor materials, and approach the process strategically.

PRESENT DATA-SUPPORTED PROJECTIONS

Investors will expect you to provide market-based projections for their return on investment and will want you to "show your math" on how you realistically arrived at those numbers. A good starting point is your base case projected return, which is basically how much the company would grow over a period of time (usually five years) if you did nothing but let it just continue on its current path.

A quick online search should reveal several templates for **leveraged buyout** financial models—acquisition with the use of debt financing—where you can plug in your assumptions and get them to spit out a return projection. Begin with your base case, which shows where the business will end up if you do nothing but allow it to remain in a steady state. You can estimate your base case scenario by modeling out what the next five years' financial performance will look like using the following assumptions:

- Projected revenue growth approximates year-over-year historical growth, removing or mitigating for any outlier years.
- Hold the profit margin flat, unless you know there will be a substantial increase in cost(s) after acquisition.
- Exit of the business (sale or liquidity event) will be at the same EBITDA or revenue multiple as your purchase multiple.
- No dividends are paid for the term of the holding period but rather accumulate for distribution at exit. There will be more on this below, in our discussion of the investor waterfall payout.

The above model can be as simple or complex as you want it to be. If you plan to involve institutional capital sources or sophisticated individual investors, your model will need to be more robust and will likely require some professional assistance from your financial advisor. Pro tip: Save your model in an editable spreadsheet, so when material changes come up in the future (such as significant revenue growth from a new product line or a drastic increase in supply costs), you can plug new numbers into your model and determine the impact on your initial projected returns.

But do not stop at the base case! Your investors will also want to see the estimated outcome of your planned value creation initiatives. These more favorable projections are referred to as the upside case or growth case and yield important metrics—discussed below—which allow you and your equity holders to compare returns across investments of different sizes, industries, and asset classes.

My philosophy on projections is to be optimistic but realistic and remember that, at the end of the day, they are just that: projections. Do your best to bridge the gap between what provides comfort to your investors but allows you to sleep at night. For the upside case, you will need to gauge the business's estimated performance under your new ownership, including

- improvements in revenue projections, from both organic (market and/or product expansion) and inorganic (acquisitive) growth;
- reductions in cost estimates due to efficiency initiatives, staffing changes, supply chain savings, or any other change that improves margins;
- the inclusion of any anticipated capital expenditures, such as new facilities or technology; and
- **exit multiple arbitrage**, which is the difference between your entry and exit multiples (for example, buying at 5× EBITDA and selling at 7× EBITDA), generated by improving the company's profitability, scale, diversification, and competitive position.

When calculating your projected returns, you may want to start with the endpoint in mind and work backward to determine the magnitude of year-over-year improvements required to accomplish your return goals. One metric to consider is the **internal rate of**

return (IRR). IRR is an annualized percentage return that can be used to compare profitability between different investments whose returns are expressed annually. For example, a private capital acquisition can frequently yield an IRR of 20 to 35 percent, compared to an annual return on the stock market of 8 to 12 percent. Many small business acquirers target an IRR in the low to mid-30 percent range, with a typical holding period of four to seven years, depending on the risk profile of the acquisition.

The other key metric of interest to investors is your equity multiple or **Multiple on Invested Capital (MOIC)**, which is your total projected return (original equity plus upside) divided by your invested capital (original equity amount). A common target is 2× to 3×, meaning that investors expect to double or triple their money over the holding period. If your projections are coming out significantly more or less than this average target, it does not necessarily mean you have done it wrong or are looking at a bad investment, but it could signal that you need to dig in deeper to find the driver(s) behind it being an outlier.

SAMPLE CALCULATIONS OF IRR AND MOIC

Let's say you have a business with a purchase price of $10 million. With an EBITDA of $2.5 million at the time of purchase, your entry multiple is 4×.

You fund your acquisition as follows:

- 60 percent is equity ($6 million).
- 40 percent is debt ($4 million). This debt is interest-only and is to be repaid in full at exit.
- The EBITDA grows from $2.5 million to $4 million over five years.
- Your exit multiple is 5.5×, so $4 million EBITDA × 5.5 = $22 million enterprise value at exit.

The cash back to equity investors can be calculated by subtracting the $4 million in debt repayment from the $22 million in sale proceeds, coming to $18 million cash returned.

The IRR comes to approximately 24.6 percent. Of note, if this deal were financed with 100 percent equity and no debt, the IRR at the same exit value would be considerably less—17.1 percent—demonstrating how strategically using debt can boost investment returns.

Now, to calculate the MOIC:

$$\text{MOIC} = \frac{\text{Total Cash Returned to Equity}}{\text{Equity Invested}} \quad \frac{\$18{,}000{,}000}{\$6{,}000{,}000} = 3.0$$

Figure 8.1: The MOIC comes to 3.0.

With 100 percent equity and no debt, the MOIC would be calculated as $22 million divided by $10 million, coming to 2.2.

Finally, before you begin pitching to investors, you will need to define your **minimum check size**, **holding period**, and the **waterfall structure**. Setting your minimum check size (the minimum investment you want from investors) may sound simple, but several considerations come into play. First, you need to balance the total capital requirement with the number of investors you want on your cap table; remember, you will be "married" to these folks for at least a few years, in sickness and in health (of your business), so shoot for a manageable number. Larger investors, such as family offices or PE funds, tend to write sizeable checks and often seek greater control and decision-making influence in return. Because of their bigger stake, they may want to negotiate key terms with you as the new owner/operator—including carried interest, employment agreements, and other governance rights.

On the other hand, smaller investors can help diversify the group that is backing you and your new business. While it might be easier to attract agreeable investors with lower minimum check sizes, managing numerous smaller checks can slow down the fundraising process and increase the burden of documentation. For HNW individuals, a minimum investment of between $50,000 and $250,000 is typical, whereas institutional investors often require a minimum of $1 million to make the deal worthwhile. In general, the cap tables for most small business acquisitions end up with between five and fifteen investors, often with a mix of institutional and individual entities.

You will also need to define your intended **holding period**, or how long you expect to retain ownership of the business, at least in its initial structure, after acquisition. For most investor-backed acquisitions, a typical holding period is assumed to be five years (with a range of three to seven years in reality), unless otherwise specified. And because potential investors' funds will be completely **illiquid** during this time frame (meaning that they will not be able to get their money out of the deal, except in extreme circumstances with significant penalties), they will be keenly interested in your **exit strategy** and timeline. Most exits include a complete or partial sale of the business to either a **strategic buyer**, usually another company in the same industry, or a **financial buyer**, such as a PE fund. In the fortunate scenario where your company has gained appropriate scale and financial success, another form of exit is going public through an **initial public offering**, which converts ownership stakes into publicly tradable shares on a stock exchange.

But what if you want to hold the asset long-term and do not wish to exit after a typical holding period? No worries—you can offer your investors the ability to cash out at a **liquidity event** after the anticipated holding period. Other than converting their equity into cash through a full exit, you can provide shareholders liquidity through **recapitalization**, which involves restructuring the company's capital stack, generally by replacing some of the existing equity with debt or new equity investors.

Lastly, another set of terms that may be negotiated during your fundraising process is how each investor will line up in the **waterfall structure**. Upon exit of the business, this tiering of your equity holders will dictate the order and magnitude of the distributions made to investors. As the name implies, think of the lump sum proceeds from a liquidity event at the top of a rocky waterfall—the payouts get thinner as the water runs down each level, until the "water" (proceeds) runs out. A basic SMB acquisition waterfall might follow something like this pattern:

- **Return of capital:** Each investor first gets back the same amount of money they originally put in.
- **Preferred return (hurdle rate):** Also referred to as the "pref," you can think of this as an investor's annual, compounded rate

of return on their invested capital, accrued over the holding period. Not to be confused with a dividend, this is paid out of the profits at exit before any carry (explained below) is distributed. SMB deals often have a range of 7 to 8 percent preferred return but can hit 10 percent or more for aggressive or risky investments.

- **Catch-up provision:** Sometimes, the general partner (GP—this will be you in a future exit of your SMB) gets first dibs on the profits, up to a predetermined threshold, before profits are widely distributed to the limited partners (LPs, the equity holders on your cap table).
- **Carried interest:** Also known simply as "carry," these are the percentages of the profits that the GPs and LPs agree to split after the preferred return is paid. A common split is 20 percent to the GPs and 80 percent to the LPs.

PREPARE YOUR INVESTOR MATERIALS

This is a lot of information to remember and keep straight, right? No worries, you will document and communicate these terms in your investor materials. Some of this will already be in your **private placement memorandum (PPM)**, a document used to share important information with investors when raising money to buy a business privately. Even if you don't have a PPM, what I've just described will need to be spelled out in your pitch deck—one of the most pivotal tools in the fundraising process.

But before we get to the full pitch deck, I want to talk about two other things you'll need: an **NDA** and a **teaser deck**. A nondisclosure agreement or NDA is just what it sounds like—a legally binding document ensuring the confidentiality of what is to be discussed.

Until this point, you may have signed NDAs, likely when you were evaluating potential deals, but you may not have developed one for yourself or your investment entity. While templates are easily found online, you should rely on your attorney to author this for you and your specific situation; they almost certainly already have a standard document that can be quickly modified to meet your needs. While rare, there is a possibility that a potential investor can use the sensitive information they learn during your pitch to compete with you or to interfere with the acquisition process and rollout.

You will also need a **teaser deck**, which is a brief presentation designed to entice potential investors to sign your NDA and learn more about your deal. It outlines key aspects of your acquisition but avoids sensitive data or detailed information, giving them just enough to encourage discussion and help them decide if they want to dig in further. You will want to give your acquisition a code name, such as Project Pharma or Project Volt. Most teaser decks are six to ten slides and cover these topics:

- **Executive summary:** A brief overview of the opportunity
- **Business overview:** A deidentified description of the company, as well as its scale and position
- **Investment thesis:** Reasons it makes for a good investment
- **Market overview:** Market trends and the competitive landscape
- **Acquisition strategy:** How the transaction and capital stack will be structured
- **Value creation plan:** Strategies for growth and an increase in valuation
- **Financial highlights:** Key metrics and generalized projections
- **Investment terms:** Details of investor participation, including the timeline

Important: I suggest doing your full pitch deck *first* and then extracting key slides and data points for the teaser deck, removing sensitive data and identifying references to the company as needed. Doing the full pitch deck first will make creating the teaser deck much easier. Which brings me to ...

THE FULL PITCH DECK

Your full **pitch deck** will be a big undertaking, as it often requires a professional-looking design, robust detail, and sophisticated models. The goal with this deck is to inspire confidence by proffering clear and compelling data that supports your investment thesis and projected returns. If you do not have a strong skill set when it comes to slide decks, consider retaining a graphic designer—or at least a savvy college student—to help professionalize your presentation, especially if you will be sending it to institutional investors. Note: Whoever you hire to help you with this practicality should sign an NDA.

Because potential investors will have already signed your NDA before receiving your pitch deck, these slides should clearly reference the company's name and contain actual performance results. Your pitch deck should be marked as confidential and distributed with caution, because of the sensitive nature of the information therein. While there are no rules on length and content, a typical pitch deck will generally run between twenty and thirty slides and contain all relevant information an investor would reasonably want to know when deciding whether to move forward.

Of course, you will need to prepare a narrative—better yet, a compelling story—to accompany these slides that will personalize your connection to the investment and demonstrate your enthusiasm for the acquisition. A well-structured pitch deck can help you organize essential data while also telling a story. I've included a quick pitch deck checklist here. For a more detailed explanation of what each of these terms means, see the pitch deck guide on my website.

PITCH DECK CHECKLIST

The following list outlines common pitch deck components for a traditional LMM business acquisition. Every target company is different, and yours may require additional content to cover special situations in your planned transaction; likewise, smaller deals will have shorter and simpler decks. Feel free to change up the order to fit your narrative, but be sure to hit the following topics:

- cover slide
- executive summary
- buyer background
- market opportunity
- details on the target company's business model
- investment thesis
- value creation strategies
- risks of the acquisition
- projected returns
- exit strategy
- valuation and deal structure
- management, transition, and governance
- investor ask
- conclusion

To download the full pitch deck checklist, visit the resources page at lisapiercey.com.

APPROACH THE FUNDRAISING PROCESS STRATEGICALLY

Once you have all of your materials, you are ready to go out to market with your fundraising efforts. Dust off your list of potential investor contacts and take a few minutes to rank each of them in tiers: A, B, or C. Your A-tier investors are those who seem to be a perfect fit for your investment criteria; they write the right-sized checks and are ready to deploy capital. B-tier investors are credible and well-capitalized but may not have experience in your investment's industry or size. Investors in the C-tier are smaller and less likely prospects but may be willing to invest in a particularly compelling opportunity. As counterintuitive as it may sound, start pitching to your B-tier investors first. This strategy helps you test and refine your presentation, gather feedback, and build momentum before approaching the A-tier. Fill the rest of your dance card with C-tier prospects as time allows.

The sequence of equity fundraising for a business acquisition typically begins with an email containing a robust and compelling description of the opportunity. This email should include your teaser deck that highlights key points of the acquisition, offering enough information to spark interest. Additionally, it is important to attach your NDA to the email or reference that an NDA will be sent shortly for an e-signature. Once the NDA is signed, you can send the full pitch deck and offer to schedule a live conversation to dive deeper into the details.

Do whatever you can to secure time for a live presentation—either virtually or in person—where you walk through the full acquisition opportunity and answer substantive questions from potential investors. The passion and enthusiasm the potential investor hears in your voice will be much harder to turn down, so do not rely on your slide deck to tell the story.

If there is continued interest, a follow-up conversation may be necessary to discuss the terms of the investment, the level of commitment, and any special requests the investor may have. After the third or fourth interaction, you should solicit a soft commitment or, at minimum, a definitive timeline for making a decision. Understandably, some investors will need to consult with their financial advisor, spouse, attorney, and/or partners, and others will want to see who else shows interest in joining the cap table before they commit. A larger investor may wish to negotiate specific terms before making a commitment. Those agreements should be formalized in a term sheet or simply documented through an email outlining the agreed-upon parameters.

Every investor is different and should be handled uniquely; if you try to force someone into your timeline, they will likely tap out. They know—and so should you—that there are plenty of other places to deploy their money. As an investor myself, when I'm being pitched a deal, there are a few things that tend to turn me off quickly. The first is being asked to make a decision on a compressed timeline—statements like "There's only one spot left" or "We need soft commits by Friday" make me question whether the process is being run thoughtfully. Second, if there's no sober discussion of risks or a downside scenario, it's hard to take the pitch seriously. Every deal has challenges, and I want to know that those challenges are being fully considered. Finally, a sloppy or incomplete deck—missing key metrics, typographical errors, or unclear deal terms—signals a lack of preparation. All of that makes it hard to build trust from the start and will make me more likely to pass.

Once the commitments start rolling in, start thinking about a closing date, usually at least three to four weeks after all financing—both debt and equity—is secured. If you have had robust interest in your acquisition and have raised more equity than you initially sought, you could encounter a situation where you are **oversubscribed**, giving you leeway to be selective about investors you want to participate, as well as the terms offered.

A more common scenario in equity fundraising is that, as the weeks pass, you find yourself close to reaching your goal but not quite there. Fundraising is emotionally draining—it often begins with encouraging momentum, only to hit roadblocks or, worse, see a major commitment drop out unexpectedly. As time progresses, multiple work streams begin to compete for your attention, from negotiating debt documents to managing legal agreements and keeping investor relations on track. The stress and sleep deprivation creep in, and it becomes increasingly difficult to keep everything moving forward while trying to pinpoint a date when it will all come together.

When you're in the throes of fundraising and things start to feel chaotic or stuck, it's important to remind yourself that this is all part of the journey. Nearly every successful fundraising process has its share of slowdowns, surprises, and stress. The key is to keep your cool, stay flexible, and push forward. Keep the conversations going and trust that consistency and professionalism will carry you through. You're probably closer to the finish line than it feels—hang in there!

Stay Gracious and Maintain Trust to Build Relationships

You will almost certainly face repeated rejection and will occasionally get ghosted, even by friends who are not comfortable turning you down directly. When you do get a no, ask for referrals to other potential investors, and if the person is an industry expert, see if they would be willing to offer advice in the future when you encounter new opportunities or challenges. Do your best to not take the rejections personally—the vast majority of investors will pass respectfully, though you may occasionally encounter slightly colder responses.

Beware of the "Nashville No," which is a firm "No" disguised as a polite excuse—because in the South, where I live, we do not want to be harsh or unpleasantly direct. Potential investors will "pass for now" on your opportunity for a host of reasons, from timing issues to a lack of team bandwidth. Often, however, this encouraging-yet-defeating feedback is accompanied by an offer to make introductions or assist you strategically after acquisition ... So take them up on it! As mentioned in the introduction to this chapter, a big part of your success will come from building relationships—and that will require staying gracious and maintaining trust.

Ultimately, the key to building trust with investors is consistent, timely follow-up. Investors are entrusting you with their hard-earned money, so it is essential to stay humble and committed to maintaining that trust through clear, organized communication. After your initial pitch, be sure to follow up promptly, with regular touchpoints to keep the conversation moving forward, but avoid overcommunicating to the point of pestering. And one more thing regarding trust: It should go without saying, but never ever fudge the numbers or present misinformation in order to secure funding. You will wind up disreputable at best, and incarcerated at worst.

Eventually, you'll land the right mix of lenders and investors and put together a capital stack that makes sense for your acquisition. And with your financing in place, you'll be ready to move on to the final milestone—closing the deal.

CHAPTER 9

THE CLOSING PROCESS AND BEYOND

"The heights by great men reached and kept,
Were not attained by sudden flight,
But they, while their companions slept,
Were toiling upward in the night."[21]

—*Henry Wadsworth Longfellow*

The weeks before closing are like those leading up to a wedding: It is an unimaginably hectic and stressful time, with a focus on staying well and keeping your cool while also buzzing with excitement and anticipation. The last few days often feel impossibly difficult with time pressures, doubts, fears, fatigue, and tons of emotions. It is a roller coaster! And if (when) you get to a point where you do not think you can take anymore, remember, this, too, shall pass. You will likely only

21 Henry Wadsworth Longfellow, "The Ladder of St. Augustine," in *The Complete Poetical Works of Henry Wadsworth Longfellow* (Houghton Mifflin, 1893), 186.

go through this one or two times in your whole life, so lean in, and as the iconic military mantra goes, "Embrace the suck!"

As your fundraising for the acquisition nears completion, the closing process kicks into high gear, and it often feels like a full-time job. At this stage, you will have to manage multiple work streams simultaneously, talk to your attorney and/or banker almost daily, and work tirelessly to close your **equity gap**—the last little bit of funding you need before having a full cap table.

The closing process is typically driven by the attorneys, as well as your lender, and you will invariably be asked to scurry around and find various pieces of obscure information for the closing documents. This is especially true if any of your funding sources participate in partnerships backed by grants or state/federal government entities. In addition to completing all of the documentation requirements, there may even be an eleventh-hour request by the seller to change one or more of the terms upon which you have already agreed. If you do get hit with one of these requests, instead of getting irritated (it can happen quickly at this point), consider any outstanding needs or wants on *your* side and ask for them in exchange—the negotiation is not over yet! When time is short and **transaction fatigue** sets in, both the seller and the buyer are ready to do what it takes to get the deal across the finish line.

In short: Be prepared for a final push that may well make you feel you are being stretched to the limit at times. Remember, most of those last-minute curveballs fade quickly once the deal is done, so take a breath and keep everything in perspective. I learned this lesson the hard way.

In the final days of an acquisition I participated in, I was unpleasantly surprised when the seller insisted on being involved in determining postacquisition roles, compensation, and incentives for existing leaders and even rank-and-file employees in the business. When first confronted with this request, I was incredulous that the seller tried to influence what I viewed as *my* soon-to-be employees and *my* intended compensation structure for them. After I pitched a small fit to the broker about the seller needing to take a step back, the broker convinced me to at least let the seller share recommendations privately, with an understanding that the final decision was mine. Thankfully, the seller provided reasonable and helpful insights and even encouraged me to push back against the lofty salary bump demanded by one executive. So, I ate my slice of humble pie—and learned that this kind of input is actually pretty common from sellers. I recommend that if you are confronted with a similar situation, you get off your high horse and consider the seller's viewpoint, even if you end up going in a different direction.

Above all, that experience taught me to keep a cool head amid the frenzied final days of a deal. Tough as it may be at times when you're exhausted and harried, maintain composure as you go through the closing process—and keep in mind that you are in the home stretch.

Phases of the Closing Process

Each business acquisition can look different, and because your transaction is unique to your specific situation, it is crucial to have trusted legal advice to guide you through the details of the closing process. While you should not rely on this guidance for legal advice, it is helpful to get a general overview of what happens in the weeks before closing, as well as the types and purposes of documents you will likely encounter.

As your fundraising draws to a close, your first phase of closing involves finalizing due diligence. This is when you will address any remaining diligence items, such as reaching out to key customers or suppliers that you have held off contacting until the deal is nearly done. It is also the time to check that the company's financials and operational metrics are updated, especially if the closing is contingent upon certain conditions being met or actions being completed.

If you have not already addressed it, another important piece is the management and employee transition. You will have certainly made verbal indications about keeping certain employees (or not), but now is the time to codify this in writing. Job offers and transition plans need to be prepared for key leaders, and retention incentives may come into play. Some employees may require new or revised employment contracts, especially if their role is critical postacquisition. In some cases, the seller may want to offer bonuses to employees who contributed significantly to the sale or transition.

When applicable, regulatory approvals may be required before the deal can officially close. Sometimes, signing the purchase agreement happens several days or even weeks before the actual closing date to allow time for things such as license transfers or other regulatory processes that can only begin once a definitive agreement is in place. In addition to regulatory or licensing agencies, be sure to check whether your contracts with suppliers, insurance companies, or accrediting bodies require notification of the change in ownership—some may require thirty-plus days of notice before closing, so you will have to account for this in the timeline.

Finally, the biggest chunk of your time in the weeks before closing will be spent negotiating and finalizing legal agreements. This includes all of the documents that will populate the **closing binder**. A comprehensive collection of all the agreements related to the acquisition, the closing binder serves as the official record of the transaction. In addition to the documentation related to the seller and the lender, you will also be preparing the necessary investor documentation and scheduling the **capital call**, which is when you formally request the invested funds be wired to your account, usually a few days to a couple of weeks before closing. Other funding-related tasks include setting up any necessary escrow accounts, scheduling outbound wire transfers, and making final adjustments to the purchase price based on real-time changes in working capital or inventory.

Here is a breakdown of common agreements that may be needed to finalize the acquisition—for a full list of documents, see the comprehensive checklist on the resources page at lisapiercey.com. Not all of these documents will be required for every transaction, but most acquisitions will include forms of the following:

- **Purchase agreement (asset or stock purchase agreement):** The primary and guiding document that spells out the terms and details of the acquisition.
- **Operating agreement:** This defines how the acquired business will be owned and managed postclose. It outlines roles, profit distributions, and decision-making authority, as well as investors' rights, protections, and return structures.
- **Financing documents:** These "debt docs" will be a book of their own! This multirecord package includes all of the agreements related to borrowing a large sum of money to finance your acquisition.
- **Disclosure schedule:** An up-to-date listing of any specific exceptions to the reps and warranties made by the seller, including outstanding liabilities, pending lawsuits or regulatory actions, key contract details, etc.
- **Closing statement (flow of funds):** This is essentially the one-pager of the math of the deal. The closing statement sometimes includes reference to, or the entirety of, the **Sources and Uses** table. This table is the central source of

truth that outlines where the funds for the purchase are coming from (the "sources," such as investor equity, bank loans, and seller financing), as well as how those funds will be spent (the "uses," including purchase price, transaction fees, and working capital).

- **Assignment and assumption agreements:** These are the documents that allow for the transfer of intangible assets, specifically intellectual property, contracts, and leases.
- **Escrow agreement:** Usually, a portion of the purchase price is held in escrow to cover working capital adjustments and any postclosing contingencies, such as pending lawsuits.
- **Employment or retention agreements:** Usually applicable, these are needed if you want key employees to stay on after the acquisition.
- **Governmental and regulatory approvals:** Licenses, permits, or regulatory approvals that are required to complete the sale are documented in this section.
- **Tax documents:** Forms and documents pertaining to the taxes surrounding the sale.
- **Lease assignment:** The leases for office space, equipment, and/or vehicles will be assigned to you with this document, including whether the arrangement(s) will continue or terminate.

Given all of these potential provisions, it is easy to see how a closing binder can add up to hundreds of pages. For my largest deal to date, the debt docs alone were 248 pages. While I felt comfortable reading and loosely interpreting many of the transaction documents, I was almost entirely out of my wheelhouse with the more complex and very technical agreements. To ensure I knew exactly what I was signing, I relied heavily on the trust I had in my legal team to comb through and translate these nuanced documents for me. Unsurprisingly, this can rack up hefty sums of legal and advisor fees, but it is money well spent. And, once the paperwork is done, you move to the most consequential and anticipated event: closing day!

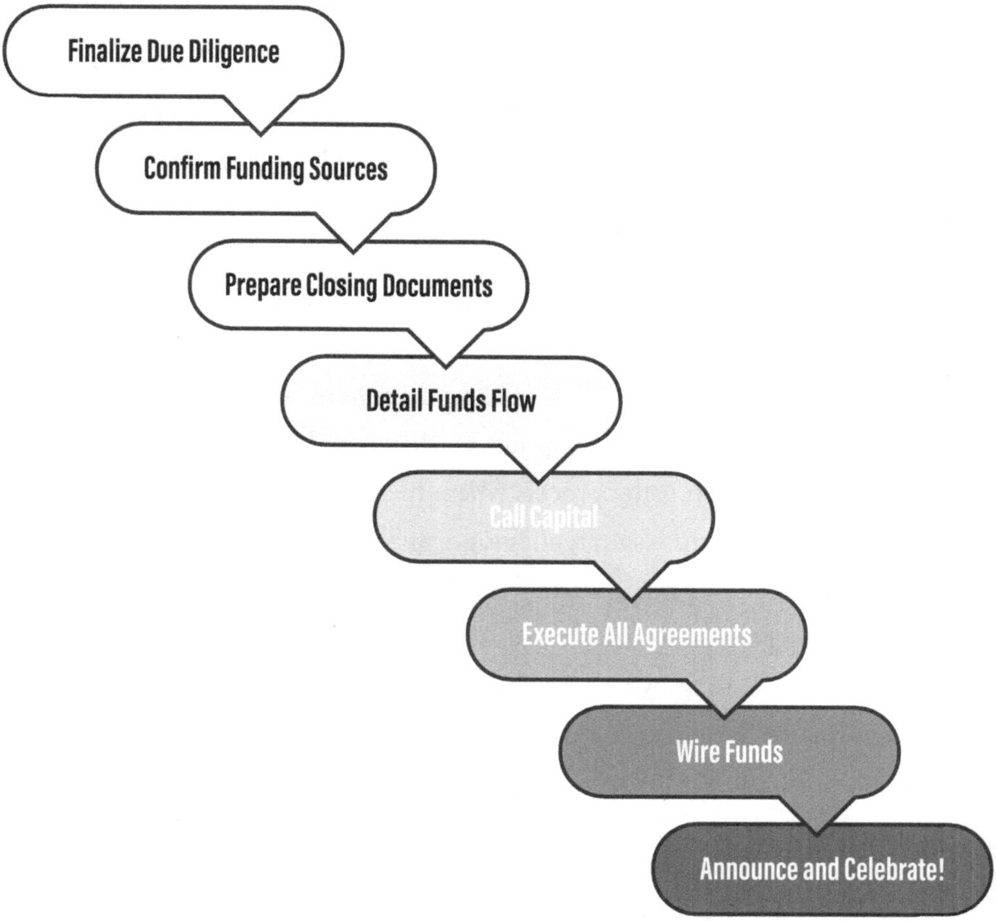

Figure 9.1: A visualization of the closing process.

Closing Day

When the big day finally comes, it will not be lost on you that closing day is a critical moment where ownership is transferred and all of the legal and financial obligations you have been discussing are executed.

Here is an overview of the activities and tasks you can likely expect to occur on closing day:

FINAL REVIEW OF CLOSING DOCUMENTS

Review and finalize all transaction-related documents, including the purchase agreement, schedules, and exhibits. Pay close attention to any last-minute inclusions or revisions. The Track Changes feature in many software programs is invaluable!

A word of wisdom: If you have held open a spot to plug in a real-time calculation just before closing, such as AR or inventory, make sure you review the seller's numbers before signing—these will most likely be included in the **closing statement**, which will be the basis of a potential postclosing **net working capital reconciliation**. This reconciliation is the process where the actual working capital at closing is compared to a target amount (known as the peg) to adjust the final purchase price if warranted. If you need more time to review, do not feel pressured to accept the closing statement as is; rather, ask to delay the closing by a day or two so you can get comfortable with what the seller has presented. Once you execute the agreement, your signature indicates acceptance of their calculation(s), which could prove difficult to revise after the deal is done.

TRANSFER OF LICENSES, PERMITS, CONTRACTS, AND INSURANCE COVERAGE

Confirm that proper notification has been made to regulatory bodies, licensing agencies, and contracted vendors in order for you to legally and contractually operate the business after acquisition. Do not wait until the eleventh hour to do so! Many entities, especially in highly regulated industries, have a specified notice period for these transfers, so you will need to account for the estimated time frames when scheduling your closing. These change of ownership requirements can range from a simple notification to a full application and approval, which can take weeks to process.

Make sure you have proper insurance coverage, which may involve reassigning existing policies, noting any postclosing changes, or securing new policies, such as directors and officers coverage or key person insurance, as required by your investors or lender(s). Additionally, any relevant assets, including vehicle titles and patent registrations, must be updated to reflect the new ownership, ensuring compliance and protection under the new management structure.

Following the signing of the purchase agreement, there are scenarios in which a **delayed closing** may occur after a planned amount of time passes. A closing may be intentionally delayed after signing the purchase agreement for a period of time to secure regulatory approvals, obtain third-party consents, or negotiate purchase price adjustments based on findings during due diligence. Other reasons might be the need to raise capital or await the outcome of a pending legal matter.

By far, the most dramatic and painful experience of the three deals I've completed happened between the signing and closing of my largest acquisition to date. Three weeks into a planned eight-week delayed closing, we encountered a pending audit that prevented the transfer of a license in the company's highest revenue state. Since the regulatory body could not give us a definitive timeline for resolution, the gut-wrenching decision was made to call off the deal— while leveraging the purchase agreement's reps and warranties—because of the seller not being able to meet the closing deliverables.

While both parties were devastated by the prospect of a failed transaction after months of diligence and expenditures, I approached the seller with the offer to operate the company as its contract CEO until the matter was resolved—credit to an insightful attorney and mentor for this stellar idea! The seller appreciated this opportunity to keep the deal alive, and my investors and I were thrilled with the prospect of spending time in the business prior to acquisition, allowing us to hit the ground running postclose.

The audit was successfully resolved over five months after encountering the licensure roadblock, and we resumed the transaction with mostly the same terms as before. And because of a couple of minor discoveries during my contracted time at the helm, I was able to renegotiate the purchase price (to my benefit) in the revised purchase agreement. Our second attempt at a delayed closing went smoothly, and the acquisition was eventually finalized approximately eleven months after the deal initially died. Moral of the story: If an unexpected barrier pops up in the process of buying a good business, find a creative way to keep the deal alive!

COMMUNICATION OF THE TRANSACTION

A clear communication strategy is essential in the final stages of a business acquisition to ensure a smooth transition and to maintain the confidence of clients and employees. Planning out how and when to share the news should be considered for each key stakeholder group, such as employees, investors, clients, and regulators, keeping everyone informed about important developments. Internal communication helps maintain employee confidence, while external messaging reassures clients and business partners about the continuity of services. Additionally, in some instances, a public notice might be required. The strategy should also address leadership changes and integration plans to avoid confusion and disruption.

When deciding on the timing of an announcement to the company's employees, consider doing this earlier in the week instead of on a Friday. While finalizing the transaction is familiar and comforting to you, it can be quite anxiety-provoking to employees, especially those who were unaware these discussions were occurring. So, instead of dropping this news on a Friday and then forcing employees to wait through the weekend to get additional information (including quelling their concerns about their jobs being cut or changed), aim to tell them on a Monday or Tuesday so they will have all week to interact with both new and old leadership and get their questions answered.

EXECUTION OF LEGAL AGREEMENTS

Now it's time to sign all of the necessary legal and financing documents. Fortunately, these signings are typically done electronically and remotely now, unless you have arranged to meet in person for more of a ceremonial physical signing. Some documents require a wet-ink signature, and in those cases, you may be able to sign a day or two in advance, with the documents held in escrow until the official closing.

Right before the documents are executed, you will likely have a **closing call**, where all parties—buyer, seller, attorneys, lenders—hop on a video or phone call to have a final conversation to confirm that closing conditions have been met, address any last-minute issues, and detail the timing and logistics of the actual closing.

TRANSFER OF FUNDS

Complete the payment of the purchase price to the seller, most commonly using a wire transfer, or any other agreed-upon payment method, and then confirm the receipt of funds by the seller. You will likely be sending other wire transfers on this date, as per your flow of funds document. These additional payments can include vendor fees, escrow account funding, and closing costs, such as legal fees, title insurance, and recording fees.

Pro tip: Gather all banking information a few days prior to closing and review it by phone with your bank on the day before closing so those wire confirmation calls do not have to occur on closing day. If your bank will allow you to confirm them beforehand, you can simply give your banker the authorization to "push the button" on the wires once the document signatures are complete. Be sure to retain the wire confirmation emails you will receive once each wire has been sent.

In addition, if your purchase agreement involves any monetary holdbacks or contingencies, an **escrow account** will need to be opened a few days before closing to hold these funds. When choosing the financial institution for this escrow account, shop around for the best savings or money market rate so the money will earn a little interest while it waits to be released. Since these are the seller's funds that are being held back, the earned interest at the time of disbursement is due to the seller. The escrow agent should be provided with the conditions for releasing the funds and advise you on the process for doing so at the appointed time.

One more note on bank accounts: After all acquisition-related funds have been disbursed at the time of closing, your SPV account will not see much action. You could close it or convert it to the business's deposit account, but another great use of this account is to convert it to an interest-bearing savings account to hold excess cash generated by the new company. Once you know your typical amount of **working capital**, or the average cash balance needed to fund day-to-day operations, you can set up an automated "sweep," where any excess cash over a certain amount is transferred to your savings account on a daily or weekly basis.

CELEBRATION OF THE ACQUISITION

After the proverbial ink is dry on the documents, take some time to celebrate the accomplishment of the months of diligence, fundraising, and negotiation it took to get here, with all the requisite stress and emotions. In addition to immediately celebrating the win (including with family members who have suffered through the transaction alongside you), be sure to schedule time in the weeks following closing to recognize and applaud the hard work of the entire team. Consider hosting a dinner, reception, or team gathering that includes your attorneys, advisors, investors, and/or company executives to show your appreciation for their efforts in the process.

In addition to potential retention bonuses that you may have offered key executives for them to stay in their current roles postclosing, it is common for the seller to acknowledge the contributions of C-suite leaders to the acquisition process by giving them a monetary bonus around the time of closing.

Congratulations! Closing day is a monumental and climactic event that requires careful planning and coordination. It is essential for all parties involved to be well prepared, ensuring that all tasks are completed efficiently and accurately to facilitate a smooth transition of ownership. And now that *you've bought the company* (!), we will touch briefly on what to expect in the first few months as the new owner.

The First One Hundred Days

Whew, you did it ... You got through the acquisition. While you are sure to feel the relief of having the transaction behind you, now the hard work begins. You've delivered the baby—now you have to raise it! Any parent knows, the tough (but oh so rewarding!) part is just beginning. In your first hundred days, there are both tactical and relational tasks to prioritize, all the while experiencing the normal feelings of being overwhelmed, overly cautious, and thoroughly confused.

From a practical standpoint, your first day as the new owner will look very similar to the first day at a new job: securing entry to the building, setting up your email, gaining access to systems, and moving into your office. In addition to the normal first-day jitters of meeting new colleagues, you will be meeting your new employees—some, for the very first time. Keep in mind that they will be more nervous than you! The best thing you can do to calm everyone's nerves is to just be present, make yourself available, and embrace your role as the "new guy." With that in mind, I suggest coming from a place of curiosity. I have always had luck playing the "I'm the dumbest person in the room" card because, in many respects, I am! Not only does this give you permission to ask questions and learn some initial, basic functions of your new business, but it also helps demystify you and your intimidating new title of owner and boss.

First things first, make sure you have immediate access to the information you might need in a crisis situation. While this is unlikely to occur in the first several weeks of ownership, it is impossible to predict when a natural disaster, a cybersecurity hack, or a key employee loss might completely overturn your new apple cart. Because it could happen anytime—and because you are now entirely responsible for the company—you should be prepared. Think about the locations, systems, and people you might need to mobilize in the event of an emergency. At minimum, this should include keys/codes to facilities (including special instructions for after-hours entry), remote access to key operational and financial systems and all bank accounts, and an updated contact list for all employees and critical external partners.

Now that you have got the emergency plans in place, let's look at the basic blocking-and-tackling functions that need to be addressed on the first day after acquisition:

- **Financial matters:** Finalize all funds transfers, including escrow accounts, and secure access to the company's bank accounts, credit cards, and financial systems.
- **Communications:** Send out a company-wide announcement about the new leadership team, including an outline of your overarching vision and immediate next steps. Hold one-to-one or small group meetings with key personnel not involved in the transaction and make yourself available to employees for both scheduled and unscheduled interactions, including sharing your contact information.
- **Technology/IT:** Work with your IT or administrative point person to gain access to all critical operational systems, confirming that you have control over essential software, servers, and databases. Review and update user access rights, ensuring that only authorized personnel have the necessary permissions. Remove system access for persons associated with the acquisition if no longer appropriate.

After you get through the first day (which hopefully included one of those cute pictures like kids do on the first day of school), your main job is to set the tone for a smooth transition and build trust with your new team. You will also use these first few days to clarify roles, learn mission-critical operational details, and ensure the continuity of processes. Toward that end, as those first days turn into the first week, there are other tasks I suggest you add to your to-do list. Here is what a first week checklist might look like:

WEEK ONE CHECKLIST:

TASKS TO COMPLETE IN YOUR FIRST WEEK AFTER CLOSING

STRATEGY

- Create a thirty-day plan, mapping out what should be accomplished in the first month to maintain momentum postacquisition.
- Introduce the concept and begin teaching the basics of any type of operational framework you plan to roll out, including identifying a regular meeting cadence and scheduling calendar blocks accordingly.

COMMUNICATIONS

- Distribute press releases and/or other public announcements to notify external stakeholders, including customers, partners, and industry bodies, about the change in ownership.
- Reach out to key customers to introduce yourself and reassure them about the health of the business. For your top clients, arrange virtual or in-person meetings to develop a personal relationship, reinforce the stability of the business relationship, and address any questions or concerns related to the transition.
    - Consider including the seller in these conversations to demonstrate a unified front and a smooth handoff.
- Notify key suppliers, partners, and allies about the transition and discuss any potential changes to collaborative agreements.

TRUST BUILDING

- Hold employee town hall meeting(s) to meet the entire team, communicate the vision, and answer questions.
- Address any known employee concerns in a transparent manner, soliciting feedback and committing to learning fully about the issue(s) before developing an action plan. Express your desire to maintain consistency in operations, with no major changes for a period of time (usually six months).

CASH FLOW

- Update banking and payment processes, mapping out the bank accounts (old versus new) where both inbound and outbound payments will be processed. Make a game plan for winding down any old bank accounts, noting that it often takes much longer than expected for customers and payors to change the banking information in their systems.
- Assess the business's cash position through a real-time review of its cash flow, financial statements, and outstanding invoices. Consider having your company's financial leader complete a thirteen-week cash flow forecast to assess near-term cash flow needs.

Now that you have gotten the first week under your belt, your nerves may start to settle a bit. The next few weeks should be dedicated to establishing a strong foundation by building relationships and gaining a detailed knowledge of daily operations. Eventually, the first week will turn into the first month, which will turn into the first quarter, which will turn into the first year ... And before you know it, your baby is celebrating its first birthday. Of course, there are quite a few things you'll have to do to make sure it reaches that auspicious day happy and healthy.

I have included checklists for your first month, first quarter, and first year after acquisition on the resources page of my website, lisapiercey.com.

From Day One to the First One Hundred Days—and Beyond

During these first few months, when you face unexpected challenges and discover new opportunities, keep your head down and continue to get to know the company's operations, culture, and market even better. You will likely feel the urge to make big changes right away, but it is still better to take it slow. Conventional wisdom asserts that new owners should not introduce significant changes for the first six months after acquisition, and although this is not an absolute rule, it does infer a longer-term approach. Remember, you are still winning trust and getting buy-in for your vision.

Personally, I have found that launching an organizational book club within the first few weeks after closing is well received among employees and serves as an effective tool on several fronts. My go-to favorite for an easy-to-read and widely applicable book is the classic *Good to Great* by Jim Collins, which frames the company you have just acquired as being really "good" but gives permission to introduce changes in the spirit of making it "great." Invite everyone in the company to participate on a voluntary basis, purchasing the book for participants and hosting a weekly thirty-minute session to discuss one chapter per week. Not only does this reinforce the good habit of regular reading, but it also serves as a nonthreatening way to build rapport with staff, unveil cultural priorities and concerns, and learn more about the business in the process. It also invites others to participate in your vision of what greatness looks like for the company.

With that said, as you are nearing the end of your first quarter, it is common to find that some parts of the business do not live up to your expectations or what was shown in the sale documents. For many, this unmet expectation comes in the form of learning that the company's technology or processes are not as sophisticated or beneficial as advertised. For others, it is the awareness that your new team may have been telling you things they think you want to hear (because they want the boss to be happy!), but perhaps they had not given you the full picture, including any bad news that you need to know. It is normal to feel disappointed or even a little duped by this realization, but recognizing the issue(s) as an opportunity for value creation (and enhancing your return on investment) offers a brighter take on the situation.

After each acquisition, I have found myself wanting to "do something" and focusing on little things I could fix quickly. In deconstructing this urge while talking with my executive coach, I realized that the months of prolonged transaction activity immediately preceding the closing had me in a short-term, task-oriented mindset, causing me to look for the quick hit of relief after checking a box off the list. Take my coach's advice, which is borrowed from the Navy SEALs: "Slow is smooth; smooth is fast." As long as the issues are not an urgent threat to the business, learn to sit with the discomfort of a growing to-do list so you can more strategically address the needs in the context of the bigger picture. And ultimately, this is all about the big picture. You were tired of sitting in the four walls of your office and running on the hamster wheel, right? Keep striving to look beyond the office walls and remember that larger vision. This is your chance to make it a reality.

RN BOR
TURAL-
BORN
RAL-NA

CONCLUSION

FINAL WORDS

***"Good planning and hard work lead to prosperity."*[22]**

—Proverbs 21:5a (New Living Translation)

At the end of your first hundred days, you will have a much clearer picture of the asset you have purchased, what needs to be done, and the possibilities that lie ahead. For most SMBs, you are likely to encounter opportunities that allow for the potential for growth, improvement, and success. You may have learned that your newly acquired business offers

- opportunities to modernize technology and build a robust data infrastructure,
- the chance to implement data-driven decision-making for more informed strategies,
- potential for upskilling staff and management to unlock untapped capabilities,
- room to enhance employees' industry and market knowledge for stronger expertise,

22 Proverbs 21:5a (New Living Translation).

- exciting possibilities to refresh marketing and branding for a renewed identity,
- the ability to streamline processes and foster a culture of efficiency and innovation,
- creative problem-solving opportunities to replace temporary fixes with sustainable solutions,
- a fresh start to establish structure and accountability, particularly in HR processes,
- an opportunity to rebuild trust by delivering on promises and creating a positive employee experience,
- a chance to address and align cultural dynamics for a unified and thriving workplace,
- the ability to establish clear communication about your vision, differentiating it from the previous ownership, and
- a proactive approach to identify and mitigate risks, ensuring a secure and stable future.

One thing is for sure: You have learned more about your new business by being in it and actively participating in its future trajectory. Resolve to keep on learning and keep on working at it. Because, like a relationship, a successful business requires care and attention if it's going to thrive.

Entrepreneurship itself is a never-ending learning process. This book only begins to cover the essentials of the buying process. To bolster your knowledge, I encourage you to read widely on the subject, consulting not only books but also blogs, podcasts, journal articles, and social media posts. A couple of now-classic books on buying small businesses are the *HBR Guide to Buying a Small Business* by renowned Harvard Business School professors Richard S. Ruback and Royce Yudkoff and *Buy Then Build* by Walker Deibel. Additionally, there are a growing number of ETA thought leaders and industry experts who consistently produce relevant SMB-related content on LinkedIn and X. You can also find more resources on my website—lisapiercey.com.

Acquiring an SMB allows for autonomy and pride of ownership, where each decision you make fuels the adrenaline of risk and offers a direct connection between actions and outcomes. Through business ownership, you are not only contributing to the financial strength of both your and your employees' families but also to the economic stability of your community and region. It is an opportunity to create a meaningful impact—and a legacy that might even be passed on to your own children one day. The journey is not just about personal growth; it is about building a future that continues to thrive long after your acquisition.

I wish you much success and pray that your path to small business ownership will be as exciting, fulfilling, and rewarding as mine has been. Leaving the familiar grind of a corporate nine-to-five can be intimidating at first. I get it. I've been there. But if you do your homework and lean on the experience of those who have walked this path before, there's every reason to believe you'll thrive. And as you start to see that you've got what it takes, you will eventually realize: You're a natural-born entrepreneur.

RN BOR
TURAL-
BORN
RAL-N